THE STRUGGLE HAS STARTED

Reflections on Makhan Singh, Kenya's Freedom Fighter and Trade Unionist, 1913 - 1973

Edited by Shiraz Durrani

Never Be Silent. Simama Imara

Published in 2024.
Vita Books.

P.O. Box 62501-00200
Nairobi, Kenya
http://vitabooks.co.ke
info.vitabske@gmail.com

ISBN 978-9914-9451-0-2 (Paper)
ISBN 978-9914-9451-1-9 (eBook)

Design and Layout by Brian Rowa
Cell: +254 723 893 350,
Email: brianrowa@gmail.com

Never Be Silent. Simama Imara

The Struggle Has Started

Reflections on Makhan Singh: Kenya's Freedom Fighter and Trade Unionist, 1913-1973

Edited by Shiraz Durrani

THE STRUGGLE BETWEEN CAPITALISTS AND WORKERS HAS STARTED IN EARNEST

Our worker comrades! Come forward! March ahead! If you do not march ahead today, then remember that you will be crushed under the heels of capitalists tomorrow. Workers should have a united stand and should stand up strongly against the capitalists so that they should not ever have the courage to attempt to exploit workers again, nor to take away workers' rights from them,

Note: The workers of M/s Karsan Ladha have gone on strike for higher wages. It has been reported that the strike situation is becoming serious. This has now become a question of life or death for workers.

-- **LABOUR TRADE UNION OF KENYA, November 29, 1936**

Never Be Silent. Simama Imara

2024

Table of Contents

ABBREVIATIONS

ANC	African National Congress
AWF	African Workers Federation (AWF
COTU (K)	Central Organisation of Trade Unions -- Kenya
CPI	Communist Party of India
CPK	Communist Party of Kenya
DTM	December Twelve Movement
EAA	East African Association
EAINC	East African Indian National Congress
EATUC	East African Trade Unions Congress
ITU	Indian Trade Union
KANU	Kenya African National Union
KAU	Kenya African Union
KFL	Kenya Federation of Labour
KFLA	Kenya Freedom and Land Army
KPU	Kenya Peoples Union
LTUEA	Labour Trade Union of East Africa
LTUK	Labour Trade Union of Kenya
MWAKENYA	Muungano wa Wazalendo Kukomboa Kenya
NAACP	National Association for the Advancement of Coloured People
NACACP	National Association for the Advancement of Coloured People
UNIA	Universal Negro Improvement Association
UWAKE	Umoja wa Wazalendo wa Kukomboa Kenya
YKA	Young Kikuyu Association

Preface

Nearly a hundred years ago, a stripling of 14 years arrived in the then Kenya Colony accompanied by his mother and sister to join his father, who was working on the railway.

Fewer tasks can be as challenging as constructing the larger than life profile of Makhan Singh: a man who saw through and instantly rejected the tokenistic colonial assignment of Indians to a class above Africans; deconstructed the hierarchical colour bar by organising trade union activities that brought the two communities together; and brought a penetrating ideological clarity to the fight for self-determination by making a demand for Kenya's independence in 1950.

Fortunately, Makhan Singh had kept biographical notes and records that preserve for all generations the contributions he made towards creating Independent Kenya. It is a salutary lesson for all those engaged in struggles that can last over generations. The seed of freedom, planted in his heart during his early years from watching the struggle for independence by the Congress of India, would make him a vision bearer for the nation he chose as his home. Makhan Singh paid a heavy price for voicing his radical vision of Kenya as an independent nation. He would pay a heavy price for his bluntness when the colonial British administration, having failed to remove him from Kenya -- ostensibly because he had been erroneously allowed to enter the country -- detained him without trial for 11 years.

The same British colonial administration had imprisoned Makhan Singh without any trial in India for six years at four detention centres -- a harbinger to his 11-year incarceration in inhospitable parts of Kenya. Given this context, and the character of the individuals who succeeded the colonial authorities, it is not surprising that the story of Makhan Singh is one of the 'submerged narratives' of Kenya.

His life and the evident impact it had on history is proof that the values and principles we adopt and live by matter. Out of the 60 years he lived, Makhan Singh gave a frenetic tenth of these to Kenya through a burst of thinking, organising and action; then he gave more than a quarter involuntarily to the British as their detainee.

Some aspects of Makhan Singh's life are described through the work his family and compatriots saw, but putting together the variegated parts of his story is neither neat nor straightforward. He was a complex man, uprooted from the place of his birth and navigating an even more complex social and political terrain convoluted by the divisive scourge of colonialism -- an exploitative capitalist system that thrived on setting people against each other. The panoply of perspectives -- from family to radical compatriot historians, playwrights, photographers, journalists, writers and librarians -- complement and complete Makhan Singh's own biographical notes, and the important material in Zarina Patel's *Unquiet: The Life & Times of Makhan Singh.*

Although it is regrettable that for over 50 years after Makhan Singh's death knowledge of his full contribution to the making of modern Kenya has been officially suppressed, and access to it denied to a significant proportion of the population, the publication of *The Struggle Has Started* secures this hero's place in collective memory. Thankfully, as historians and archeologists have helped us to discover, it is not possible to permanently erase history. A few artifacts -- physical and ideological -- have piqued the curiosity of younger generations to seek out the true history of their existence. The essays in this book continue that pursuit for a fuller understanding of that past.

The ideological vision Makhan Singh bequeathed Kenya continues to be an important touchstone for testing the integrity of our independence. The differentiated treatment of persons, religions, races, communities and regions that so rankled Makhan Singh continues to be brought into sharp relief over the years as Kenya navigates its nationhood.

Kwamchetsi Makokha

Editor's Note: Makhan Singh Is as Relevant Today as He Was in His Time

Shiraz Durrani

Since Vita Books published the book, *Makhan Singh: A Revolutionary Kenyan Trade Unionist* in 2015, Makhan Singh, trade unions and what they stand for have become even more relevant to events in Kenya. This is mostly due to the rising class consciousness in Kenya, which has led to an increasing militancy, especially among the youth who have been active not only on the streets but have taken up study and learning of history and ideology to guide their actions. At the same time, while the docile Central Organisation of Trade Unions (COTU) has been getting ever closer to the ruling class and has all but abandoned the cause of working class, workers have taken up the challenge and strikes have gone up.

As a result, non-union resistance for political demands have brought the country to an almost standstill and paralysed the government machinery. Some aspects of the recent resistance are captured in Durrani (2024 a[1], b[2], c[3]). It will be observed that this resistance, unlike the Mau Mau one, is not led by working class. Indeed, working class, as a class, is noticeably absent from the resistance. Perhaps because of this, there is a lack of clarity about ideology or organization, both of which are necessary tools for successful resistance. This is explained

1 Durrani, S. (2024a): Historical Perspective on the Resistance of Gen Z in Kenya. Countercurrents.org. Available at: https://countercurrents.org/2024/07/historical perspective-on-the-resistance-of-gen-z-in-kenya/

2 Durrani, S. (2024b): People's Resistance to Capitalism and Imperialism in Kenya — Then and Now. Available at: https://countercurrents.org/2024/07/peoples-resistance-to capitalism-and-imperialism-in-kenya-then-and-now/

3 Durrani, S. (2024c): What Next for Resistance in Kenya as the Comprador Government Increases Repression? Available at: https://countercurrents org/2024/08/what-next-for-resistance-in-kenya-as-the-comprador-government increases-repression/

further in the last article mentioned above:

> Yet they [the resistance] face daunting tasks. For one, they do not have the support of organised labour nor of organised peasant movements. There is thus a danger that they may be isolated by the comprador government and killed or disappeared or injured one by one. They have no organised defence to meet the organised assaults from Ruto, who has time to see the resistance dwindle and die out. He can wait months or years if necessary, while the resistance has to struggle not only against state resistance but also for their daily survival. The resistance is distributed evenly around the country, which has the advantage of spreading out the enemy forces. But it also means that it is difficult to get support for those under attack from a united national force.

> The danger in the current situation in Kenya is perhaps similar to that in Bangladesh, which, as Isaac (2024)[4] says, faces danger because of the lack of the very aspects that are central to Makhan Singh's thoughts and actions:

> The major problem, VJ Prashad, says, is that the students have no program. However, they do – the problem is that it has no class consciousness. At a webinar on August 14 organised by the Center for Political Education, leaders of the students, garment workers and other activist groups in Bangladesh described their goals. They all called for an end to fascism, defined as a lack of free speech, the ability of rulers to murder with impunity, and discrimination based on race and religion. They all called for free elections, multiple parties, representatives of labour in government and more civil rights. *None mentioned capitalism or the economic system as a target for change or even seemed to be aware of the dynamics of capitalist power [Emphasis added].*

Durrani (2024c) made similar comments about Kenya:

> The resistance has not openly declared its vision of a Kenya should Ruto and his system be defeated. Mau Mau declared boldly their aim of 'Land and Freedom'. The underground

4 Issac, Elleen(2024). Bangladesh: Another Seismic Struggle That Will Not Bring System Change. Available at: https://countercurrents.org/2024/08/bangladesh-another seismic-struggle-that-will-not-bring-system-change/

> December Twelve Movement and Mwakenya issued their Programmes and aims; the Kenya People's Union sought socialism. This helped to energise and activate those who were not part of these movements. In contrast, the present resistance has not set out a clear vision that can help workers and peasants to support them and become part of the resistance movement.

It is at such time of a lack of clarity about a vision for the future that a study of Makhan Singh and the role of a radical trade union movement are most needed. And yet, it is not that there is no awareness of the danger that capitalism and imperialism pose for the country, as pointed out by Durrani (2024c):

> At the same time the ideological struggle needs to be kept at the forefront. Only socialism can meet the demands of resistance. Only a just land policy can satisfy workers and peasants. There is no shame in proclaiming socialism as the aim of resistance as capitalism has failed working people in every country it has captured. That way, they stand to get support from socialist forces around the world too. The struggle in Kenya is not an isolated one. It is part of the struggle for socialism, justice and equality waged all around the world. It is easier today than was the case for Mau Mau to establish friendly links with those in similar struggles around the world.

It is important to study the trade union history and the work of Makhan Singh, Bildad Kaggia, Pio Gama Pinto and other trade unionists to learn the lessons that their successes and failures can give for today's resistance. And that has exactly been happening in Kenya as various groups and movements conduct study sessions on many relevant subjects, including trade union studies. Many have, moreover, undertaken the online study courses on Marxism and trade union studies run by the Marx Memorial Library in London. Indeed, it was for some of these and similar courses that Vita Books published its latest book, *Trade Union Studies in UK and Kenya.*[5]

5 See: https://www.africanbookscollective.com/books/trade-union-studies-in-the-uk-and kenya

It is instructive to see the Kenya essays in this book:

- The role of Trade Unions under capitalism and imperialism in Kenya.
- Trade Unions, Power and Politics in Kenya: No Politics, No Power!
- Trade Unions are the Future of Kenya.
- Capitalist Exploitation Entrenched in Kenya.
- What Role Did Trade Unions Play in the Struggle for Independence in Kenya?
- Trade Unions in Kenya and Britain in a Changing World.
- Prospects for Trade Unions in Kenya under Capitalist Onslaught.
- Trade Unions as the Motive Force for Resistance.
- Reflections on the Revolutionary Legacy of Makhan Singh in Kenya.
- Tunakataa! Saying 'No' to Capitalism and Imperialism in Kenya.
- Capitalism, The Prison Without Walls.
- Why Study Socialism?
- Land Is the Key Issue in Kenya.

- Fight Capitalism, Fight Imperialism by Any Means Necessary
- Is the Left Dead in Kenya?
- The Kenya Resistance Archives Adds the Missing Links to the History of Kenya.
- Kenya and Palestine Are Among the Victims of the Imperialist Power Games.
- The Struggle for Palestine is the Struggle of Working People.

The essays were written in response to the situation in Kenya and earlier versions were initially published in countercurrents.org.[6] They thus reflect the contradictions in the Kenyan society between working class and the comprador bourgeoisie and imperialism. As will be noticed, one of the essays is on Makhan Singh, *Reflections on the Revolutionary Legacy of Makhan Singh in Kenya.* It provides some reflections on why Makhan Singh is still relevant in Kenya. The essay summarises the role of Makhan Singh:

> Makhan Singh played a crucial role in Kenyan people's struggle against colonialism and imperialism. His was not a narrow perspective of gaining a limited political independence under imperialism. He saw the economic as well as political liberation of working people and the achievement of a society based on the principles of social justice and equality as the ultimate goals of trade union and the nationalist struggles. He saw the need for achieving the economic and political rights of working people who had been marginalised by colonialism, imperialism and, ultimately by capitalism, as the primary goal for people of Kenya. His base for achieving his goals was the trade union movement, which he did much to organise and radicalise along class lines. He realised that the economic demands of working people could be met only on the basis of becoming active in the political, as well as economic, field. He was among those Kenyans who saw clearly what the needs of the time were. He devoted his life to developing and committing himself totally to a vision of a society that was fair and just for working people. He helped set up an appropriate organisational framework – in trade unions and in the political field – as a way of ensuring the achievement of his vision. He developed appropriate forms of communication to raise class consciousness among people. This ensured that people understood the working of capitalism

6 These are available at: https://countercurrents.org/author/shiraz-durrani/

> and took necessary action at different stages of their struggle. He lived by the principles he believed in, making sacrifices that very few people were – or are — ready to make (pp. 202-203).

This book then adds many details on the life and work of Makhan Singh and the trade Union movement. Amarjit Chandan, for example, provides details on Makhan Singh's ideological commitment to communism, which influenced his entire life:

> Makhan Singh (1913--1973) a whole-timer of the CPI [Communist Party of India] during 1939--1947, contributed significantly to the theoretical work of the party. He spent his time in translating Marx's *Das Kapital* into Punjabi in the Gurmukhi script. In 1942, Jagjit Singh Anand, an editor of *Jang-e-Azadi,* the CPI organ, received Makhan Singh's Punjabi translation of *Dialectical Materialism*, a chapter in *Das Kapital.* In his memoir, Anand recalled his deep impression of Makhan Singh's nuanced grasp of Marxist theory as well as his mastery of the Punjabi language.

The early life of Makhan Singh in India provides details which informed his outlook and work during his time in Kenya. His central message is contained in one of the pamphlets issued during a strike in 1936:

> Our worker comrades! Come forward! March ahead! If you do not march ahead today, then remember that you will be crushed under the heels of capitalists tomorrow. Workers should have a united stand and should stand up strongly against the capitalists so that they should not ever have the courage to attempt to exploit workers again, nor to take away workers' rights from them — Labour Trade Union of Kenya leaflet. November 29, 1936.

Thus, issues of capitalism and working-class struggles were at the centre of his thoughts and action. In brief, his contribution can be summarised as follows:

- He inked economic & political struggles.
- He linked worker & TU struggles with political & national struggles.
- He showed the importance of ideological clarity and worker organization.

- He showed the need for effective communications strategy.
- He demonstrated the need for international solidarity.
- He did all this in action, with commitment & made personal sacrifice.

These are lasting lessons for Kenyans and all struggling people in Africa today. This book helps to keep his ideas and actions alive for a new generation of activists.

Makhan Singh: Autobiography of the Well-known Trade Unionist Leader

The huts at Maralal where the Communist leader Makhan Singh was detained.

COMRADE MAKHAN SINGH'S HUNGER-STRIKES FOR RELEASE OF JOMO KENYATTA AND HIS COLLEAGUES

(By MAKHAN SINGH)

The imprisonment and detention of our great leader Jomo Kenyatta and other detainees and restrictees was the biggest attack of the imperialists and colonialists that was made to crush our struggle for independence.

The heroic resistance of our people of the onslaughts of the imperialists has ultimately defeated one of the biggest imperialist powers in the world and has won our complete independence. In this resistance no small part was played by the struggle of the political prisoners, detainees and restrictees to defeat the efforts of the colonialists which were aimed at breaking their revolutionary spirit, "rehabilitating" them and prolonging their confinement for as long as possible.

Read in these pages the story of the beginnings and growth of the Movement in Kenya.

Comrade Makhan Singh Makian Singh was born on December 27, 1913, at Gharjakh, a small village in India (now in West Pakistan) in a poor but deeply religious carpenter family. His father Mr Sudh Singh came to Kenya in July 1920 to work for the Railway while Makhan Singh remained in his village with his mother, Isher Kaur, for education. During his school days in India, Makhan Singh's mind was influenced by the teachings of Sikhism and Sikh history and also by the Congress struggle for freedom of India under the leadership of Mahatma Gandhi.

With his mother and sister, Makhan Singh came to Kenya in May 1927, and continued his education in Nairobi, passing the London Matric Exam. in 1931. He had a burning desire to go abroad for further studies, but his father's financial condition did not allow this.

During the period of his schooling in Nairobi, Makhan Singh continued taking interest in world events and was influenced by the workers' and peasants' movement (both communist and socialist) and trade union struggles. At this time he also commenced composing and reciting poems in Punjabi on religious, social and political subjects, with emphasis on the struggle for freedom.

In June 1931, after completing his education, Makhan Singh began working in his father's printing press, which he had started in that month. Here he commenced a serious study of political literature of all types. On January 20, 1934, he married Satwant Kaur in India and they had two sons and a daughter.

In March 1935, he was elected Secretary of the Indian Trade Union, which had just then been formed by some Railway and other Indian artisans. In the following month, he along with others induced the Indian Trade Union to change its name to the Labour Trade Union of Kenya and to open its doors to all workers irrespective of race, religion, colour or creed. He became the first General Secretary of the union, working in an honorary capacity. For his livelihood, he worked in the printing press. He remained General Secretary until August 1949, when he was elected President.

The major events that took place in the history of the Union up to the end of 1939 were all under his tenure as General Secretary.

In 1935, the Union initiated the campaign to induce the Railway authorities to revert to their previous permanent status all those artisans who were made temporary employees during the years of the Great Depression. Ultimately they were restored to their former permanent status. In September and October 1936, the Union conducted a campaign for eight-hour work days, and was successful in achieving it in Nairobi and several other parts of Kenya.

In April and May 1937, the Union by means of an organised strike-action was able to achieve an increase in wages ranging from 15 per cent to 25 per cent at several work sites in Nairobi. The result of the victory was that the Union's membership rose to about 2,500 in all the main towns of Kenya and Uganda. Another result was that the government came to the conclusion that the Trade Union Movement in Kenya had come to stay and that a Trade Union legislation was necessary. A Trade Union Bill was published in the middle of May 1937, when the strike was still continuing and it became an Ordinance in August. The Union was registered under it in September 1937.

During 1938, the Union established relations with the British Trades Union Congress, South African Trades and Labour Council and the International Labour Office.
The Union organised a Workmen's Compensation Conference to inform the Kenya government of the necessity of workmen's compensation legislation. It was brought into effect in 1946.

The Union made representations to the Uganda government when expressing its views on the Uganda Labour Inquiry Committee Report, that the difficulty in obtaining African labour for industrial concerns could be overcome only by increasing wages and improving other conditions of employment.

The third Conference of the Union held at the end of July 1939 was attended, for the first time, by a large number of African workers, and two prominent Africans, Jesse Kariuki and George K Ndegwa, were elected to the Executive Committee of the Union, the first as the Union's Vice-President, and the second as member of the Committee.

A few days later the Mombasa African workers went on a general strike. The Union held a mass meeting attended by African and Asian workers to express solidarity with the strikers. A similar meeting was held when Tanga workers went on strike. After the Mombasa strike, which lasted for about 10 days, the government appointed an Inquiry Committee. The Union, at the beginning of October 1939, submitted a Memorandum by the General Secretary demanding that a minimum wage should be introduced in Kenya and it should be based on necessities of the family and not of the individual. The Union suggested Sh50 as a minimum wage on the basis of 1939 prices. The prevailing wage for African workers at that time ranged from Sh10 to Sh15.

By this time the Second World War had already started and the government did not like the activities of the Union or of its General Secretary, Makhan Singh, especially the shoulder-to-shoulder struggle by African and Asian workers. During this period, Makhan Singh, in addition to his Trade Union activities, had become active in the East African Indian National Congress and the Indian Youth League. He became a member of the Congress Standing and Executive Committees in 1938, and took an active part in all the campaigns of the Congress especially on the issues of racial discrimination and the White Highlands.

In 1939, Makhan Singh was appointed Secretary of the Indian Youth League, the organisation that had previously played an important part in shortening the working hours of shop assistants throughout Kenya and was now active in encouraging the activities of gymnasiums and adult education. Towards the end of December 1939, Makhan Singh left for India to study working class conditions and the functioning of Trade Unionism in Bombay and Ahmedabad. There, he took part in India's freedom struggle and participated in the Independence Day celebration on January 26, 1940, and in the first week of March addressed a large mass meeting of about 30,000 Bombay workers and strikers. A few days later, he attended the Ramgarh Session of the Indian National Congress as an African delegate. This session gave full authority to Mahatma Gandhi to carry out Satyagraha when he deemed it necessary.

With the intensification of the freedom struggle and the working class movement, the imperialist rulers began arresting and detaining prominent leaders and workers throughout India. On May 5, 1940, Makhan Singh was arrested at Ahmedabad on the orders of the Central Government under the Defence of India Rule and detained in the historic Sabarmati Jail. No charges were brought against him and he was subsequently detained in the Lahore Fort, Mazafforgarh Jail, Deoli Detention Camp and Gujrat Jail. During his detention, he came into contact with communist, socialist and other revolutionary leaders from all over India. In October and November 1941, he was on hunger strike along with more than 160 other detainees in Deoli Detention Camp resulting in a radical improvement in the conditions under which the detainees were kept thereafter.

Makhan Singh was released from detention in July 1942 and immediately an internment order was served upon him restricting him within the limits of village Gharjakh. He remained under restriction until January 18, 1945 when he was unconditionally released. Thus, he remained under detention and restriction in India for more than four-and-a-half years. He then began working as a sub-editor of *Jang-I-Azadi*, the weekly organ of the Punjab Committee of the Communist Party of India, in which role he continued up to the end of July 1947. He left for Kenya in the first week of August 1947. One main aim of Makhan Singh's life, the freedom of India, had been achieved.

Makhan Singh arrived in Nairobi on August 22. Five days later, a quit order was served upon him by the government of Kenya. It asked him to leave Kenya within 30 days as, according to government, he had previously, in May 1947, been declared a, prohibited immigrant and had been allowed to enter Kenya by an "oversight." He declined to obey the order and was prosecuted.

The Court acquitted him and the government could not deport him. No official reason was given by the Kenya government for its action against him, but it was revealed in the House of Commons that he had been declared a prohibited immigrant on account of his activities when he was previously in Kenya. After his acquittal, Makhan Singh resumed his political and trade union activities.

In December 1947, Makhan Singh was one of the active organisers of the Kenya Youth Conference and was elected one of its three vice presidents.

He resumed his active part in the East African Indian National Congress and was one of its leading campaigners during the May 1948 Legislative Council elections when the Congress put up its own candidates. In June, he went on a fast to protest against the government policy of dividing the Indian voters roll on religious basis and against the policies of communal leaders. In August 1948, at the Mombasa session of the Congress, he was elected to the Standing and Executive Committees of the Congress.

The following month, Makhan Singh, as General Secretary of the Labour Trade Union of East Africa, called a Cost of Living and Wages Conference, which was attended by representatives of several unions. The main significance to this conference was that African and Asian trade unionists had met together independently of the Labour Department and had unitedly discussed the burning questions facing the workers and decided to act together in the future.

The government did not like Makhan Singh's activities and on October 5, 1948, he was arrested on a warrant to deport him out of Kenya. The government did not succeed as the Supreme Court (Justice de Lestang) ruled that Makhan Singh being a permanent resident of Kenya could not be declared a prohibited immigrant and, therefore, could not be deported. He was set free within two weeks of his arrest.

At that time the Indian community in Kenya was going through a serious political crisis. Makhan Singh wrote an article (*Daily Chronicle*, 12/2/1949) to show the way forward. He said: "The main task before us is to forge a strong unity among ourselves and with Africans for the common cause of democratic advance in this country". He defined the common roll as follows:

> A drive for the establishment of a democratic government in Kenya with equal franchise, adult suffrage and common roll for all …

The tasks he suggested were these: "Organise joint fronts of Indian Associations, African Political Unions, Pakistani Organisations, Trade Unions, Chambers of Commerce, Youth Leagues, and other influential organisations for common problems. Form Trade Unions, consisting of all workers, united Chambers of Commerce of both Indian and African traders and united Youth Leagues. Establish common high schools where possible. Learn the language of the people -- Swahili. Teach the best of your culture ... This way lies our salvation and this is the way out."

During 1949, Makhan Singh, along with other African and Asian trade unionists, organised a Central Organisation of Trade Unions, the East African Trade Unions Congress. With Fred Kubai as President, he became its General Secretary. The Congress helped in coordinating the activities of trade unions and in conducting the joint struggles of African and Asian workers for better conditions of employment.

On Sunday April 23, 1950, Makhan Singh moved an addendum to a resolution about the constitutional changes in Tanganyika in a mammoth mass meeting held in the Kaloleni Social Hall, Nairobi, under the joint auspices of Kenya African Union and East Africa Indian National Congress. The addendum called upon the British Government to grant complete independence to East African territories at an early date. This was the first time in the history of East Africa when a resolution of complete independence was proposed and adopted.

On May 1, Makhan Singh wrote, "The call of May Day 1950, the middle of the twentieth century, is that the workers and the peoples of East Africa, should further strengthen their unity, should become more resolute and thus speed up the movement for freedom of all workers and peoples of East Africa."

In the evening, representatives of all trade unions met under the auspices of the East African Trade Unions Congress to celebrate May Day. They pledged to build a strong trade union movement and to fully support the Kenya African Union and the Indian Congress in carrying out the resolution of achieving complete independence for the East African territories.

The rulers in Kenya did not like the growing struggle for independence and the build-up of a strong trade union movement. On Monday, May 15, 1950, Makhan Singh and Fred Kubai were both arrested. Their arrest was followed by a protest general strike of workers in Nairobi and adjoining areas. Its main demands were the release of the arrested leaders, complete independence of East African territories and a minimum wage of Sh100 per month. (The minimum wage at that time was about Sh40). The general strike was unprecedented in the history of East Africa. It lasted for 10 days.

Proceedings were brought against Makhan Singh in the Supreme Court of Kenya for obtaining a recommendation that a restriction order be issued against him. Allegations against him were made in connection with his trade unions activities as General Secretary of the East African Trade Unions Congress, expression of political views in the course of the national struggle for freedom and his being a communist. Makhan Singh adopted an honest political attitude about the allegations. While it was the contention of the Crown that his activities were undesirable, not criminal, he stated that all these activities were justified in the circumstances. The Supreme Court Judge (Justice RS Thacker) recommended in his judgment that the government of Kenya should make a Restriction Order against him. On June 5, 1950, the Governor-in-Council made the Restriction Order against Makhan Singh and he remained restricted for about 11 and a half years at Lokitaung, Maralal and Dol Dol up to the October 22, 1961, when he was unconditionally released. During the restriction, pressure was exerted upon him to force him to either leave Kenya or change his attitude; Makhan Singh did neither.

On the day of his release, he openly declared that he was still a communist and would continue his political and trade union activities. He added: "The duty of all freedom loving peoples in Kenya is to unite under the leadership of Jomo Kenyatta for immediate independence."

In November 1961, he resumed his political and trade union activities. He joined the Kenya Freedom Party, an associate organisation of the Kenya African National Union. He resumed his membership of the Printing and Kindred Trade Workers' Union (of which he is one of the founders). He was elected Chairman of the Legislative Committee of the Kenya Federation of Labour (KFL) and was a KFL representative on the tripartite Committee, which drafted Kenya's Industrial Relations Act in 1962.

On October 21, 1962, Makhan Singh joined Kenya African National Union when its doors of membership opened to all irrespective of race, colour or creed. (Kenya Freedom Party voluntarily dissolved itself a few days later.)

In March 1963, Makhan Singh was granted the certificate of Permanent Residence after a long struggle of 16 years since 1947. Since his release, he actively worked for the unity of the national movement through KANU and for unity of the trade union movement through KFL and for their mutual unity, cooperation and solidarity with the National Government under the premiership of Jomo Kenyatta.

Kenya was now nearing the attainment, on December 12, 1963, of the second main goal of Makhan Singh's life — the complete independence of East Africa.

Through KANU and KFL, Makhan Singh was active in the struggle for building up a strong, united, democratic African Socialist Kenya, East Africa and ultimately the whole of Africa.

Introduction to Makhan Singh's Autobiography

Pheroze Nowrojee[7,8]

This publication sets out the brief autobiography of Makhan Singh, which he wrote in the third person in 1963 for publication in a book to celebrate the imminent independence of Kenya. The document is from the archives of Makhan Singh's family and is in his own handwriting.

The document is reproduced here in facsimile and transcribed into printed form; with minimal editing. This is an important document, for in the format of a brief autobiography this critical figure in the struggle against colonialism, imperialism, and imposed rule reveals what he himself considered the key steps in that journey, both for himself and for the Kenyan freedom movement.

In the space of five months between January and May 1950, Makhan Singh changed the direction of the political movements in Kenya, from seeking greater participation within colonial rule, to independence and the ending of colonial rule. His message to all East Africans was, "The only solution is the complete independence of the East African Territories." The foundations he laid made it possible for the trade unions to become carriers of nationalism and demands for freedom throughout the period of the Emergency, despite its numerous restrictions.

The colonial government first sought to deport him. When that failed, it brought proceedings in May 1950 to obtain a restriction order against him. In those proceedings, Makhan Singh set out his political beliefs

7 Pheroze Nowrojee, Co-Chair, Asian African Heritage Trust, January 2015.

8 Reproduced from *Makhan Singh: The Autobiography of Makhan Singh and Documents Relating to His Release.* (Nairobi, Asian African Heritage Trust, 2015). The Editor would like to thank the Asian African Heritage Trust for permission to reproduce this article.

and the direction he sought for his country. He does not present these in this brief autobiography; they can be found in full in Zarina Patel's biography *Unquiet: The Life and Times of Makhan Singh* (Nairobi, Kenya Human Rights Commission, 2006).

The significance of those proceedings can also be gauged from their role as a rehearsal for the legal proceedings that followed two years later at Kapenguria in 1952 -- 1953. The judge who tried Makhan Singh and ordered him into restriction was the same judge who tried and imprisoned Kenyatta, Kaggia, Oneko, Karumba, Ngei, and Kubai at Kapenguria -- Mr Justice Ransley Thacker. The prosecutor against Makhan Singh was likewise the same person who prosecuted the Kapenguria Six -- Deputy Public Prosecutor Anthony Somerhough.

Makhan Singh was sent into detention on June 5, 1950 and remained in detention for 11 years till October 22, 1961, in remote and inhospitable locations at Lokitaung, Marsabit, Maralal and Dol Dol.

Makhan Singh, throughout his political activity and writing, emphasised key issues: strong national unity for the common cause of democratic advance in Kenya; a strong trade union consciousness and movement; and the necessity of forging a democratic nation. He thereby foresaw the areas that could go wrong in the years after independence. And indeed these came to pass: disunity among the people; an emasculated· trade union movement; and the loss of the democratic gains of the freedom struggle.

The extant manuscript of Makhan Singh's autobiography is not complete. But the text was completed later for the printing of the 1963 book. Fortunately, among Makhan Singh's records were found a proofed copy of his pages as they would appear in the book. These pages carry corrections in Makhan Singh's own handwriting, and thus confirm the full text.

As the new government in 1963 moved away from the ideals of the freedom struggle, Makhan Singh remained consistent in his beliefs in social justice, as did Jaramogi Oginga Odinga, Bildad Kaggia, Pio Gama Pinto, JD Kali, and others. Their consistency was not in vain. It gave inspiration to the generations that followed in resisting the repression of the years from 1964 to 2010. The new Constitution of 2010 vindicated Makhan Singh and them all, embodying "human dignity, equity, social justice, inclusiveness, equality, human rights, nondiscrimination and protection of the marginalised" in Kenya's national values (Article 10). Makhan Singh is thus one of the architects of the new Constitution.

The lesson of Makhan Singh's struggles and of those for the new Constitution is that freedom has to be fought for again and again, and restored again and again whenever power turns into oppression, no matter how many times that happens. And the restoration of freedom always calls for the measure of courage, perseverance, and consistency that were so fully exemplified for us in the life of Makhan Singh.

Why Makhan Singh's Work Was Not A Sacrifice

Manmit S Jabbal[9]

While much has been written about Makhan Singh's role in co-founding the Kenya Trade Unions in 1949, along with Fred Kubai, many writers and scholars have portrayed my grandfather, Makhan Singh's contribution as a sacrifice on his part. Some have argued that he deserved more recognition than he received in his lifetime. But he wasn't just fighting for better working conditions; he saw it as a crucial step towards achieving independence for all Kenyans. This was the principal cause that drove him. It was his calling, and the devotion towards articulating the step he took was his chosen path towards this cause.

I wasn't even born when all this was happening and was only seven when he passed on but I first came to learn about his years in politics when listening to my grandmother's thoughts about her experiences trying her best in caring for her family. She would tell me about his long hours away with his associates -- probably articulating ideas on how to change the ways of the British for the betterment of the common workers. My own understanding of his work comes mostly from what others have written about him. However, my understanding of his character, personality and resolve to make a difference comes from what I have learned from my father, Hindpal Jabbal and my grandmother, Satwant Kaur.

Reading about trade unions in Kenya, I learned that leaders like Makhan Singh used these platforms to raise awareness about colonial

9 Manmit Jabbal is the only one of Makhan Singh's eight grandchildren who still resides in Kenya. He is an interior architect who runs a well-known design firm in Nairobi. He is passionate about his grandfather's work and has spent years studying Makhan Singh's huge archive of digitised documents. Manmit believes that his grandfather's work offers valuable lessons for future generations of activists and change makers.

injustices and advocate independence. Strikes and protests, organised by trade unions, often had broader political ramifications, challenging colonial authority and garnering international attention to the struggle for independence. His emphasis on multiracial unity within the trade union movement was crucial. It countered the British divide-and-rule tactics and fostered a sense of shared purpose among different ethnic groups in the fight for independence. Everything he did was simply a path towards this.

His resolve to strive for justice earned Makhan Singh the unenviable tag of “the longest-detained prisoner in Kenya” during the independence struggle, spending over a decade in detention. This shows his unwavering commitment to the cause and his willingness to serve his life’s calling. He willingly gave up his own personal comforts and those of his family. This would only be considered a sacrifice if it had come at the expense of something else. But there was nothing else. This was his life, his whole life, and he pursued it with every ounce of his focus.

Would anyone put a price to the devotion of a good army General towards his men or perhaps a devotee to his or her mentor or guru in serving the greater good? There is no difference between my grandfather’s devotion to his life’s focus and that of any army General’s towards his country’s cause or a true disciple’s towards his guru’s cause. Would such a person be motivated by a recognition for his or her devotion? His or her only reward would be to see that the greater cause is realised.

Our grandfather’s reward was witnessing Kenya’s independence, and earlier, India’s. From what we learned of him, this was all he ever wanted or wished for. This fulfilled his life’s calling.

His descendants will forever be inspired by his resolve to remain devoted to his focus and that he lived to see his vision materialise. Not a single one of his descendants ever refers to his work as a sacrifice. Therefore, I urge writers and scholars of Makhan Singh’s work to put aside any notion of the word “sacrifice” when describing Makhan Singh’s work and encourage you to consider words like, “calling” or “devotion” towards what in his mind was the only cause which mattered.

February 11, 2024

An Inter-Generational Conversation

Inderjit Kaur Gill interview with Gouri Sharma

GS: We have a shared history in Kenya -- my father and all his family, including his mother, were all born there. And his maternal uncle, DK Sharda, was a journalist and critic of the British colonial rulers who edited the 'Daily Chronicle', among others. Last December (2023) marked 60 years since the end of British rule in the country. Did you observe it, or did it resonate with you in any way? Do you talk about your father and his role in the country with your grandchildren?

IG: I didn't mark it in any way, it wasn't something that I really took notice of. I've got one grandson who is only two-and-a-half years old and one granddaughter who is 12 years old. She recently did our family tree so I brought up my family then. Life got busy for me after I left Kenya in 1968, pursuing further studies and raising my own family, but my elder brother Hindpal Singh Jabbal and his younger son still live there so there are some links. Generally, though it's not a place I'm closely connected with or visit much these days.

GS: To tie in with the anniversary, I wrote a piece on the life and legacy of Pio Gama Pinto[10]. Given his hugely important role in Kenyan history and the independence struggle, I was extremely surprised at how little is known about him outside of particular community and academic circles. With regard to your father's story, how well would you say the work he did is known among a wide group of people beyond those closest to him?

IG: His story simply doesn't exist outside of certain circles and I think it fits into how little is still known about British colonies and their history. It hasn't been transmitted to younger generations, and this applies not just in Kenya but in India too -- aside from one play that has been done on my father in Punjab, it's a relatively unknown story there. The first generation who arrived in the UK in the 1960s were inevitably occupied by settling into the new country and raising a family. These

---

10 Pio Gama Pinto -- The Indian journalist who joined Kenya's independence fight https://www.aljazeera.com/features/2023/12/12/pio-gama-pinto-the-indian-journalist-who-joined-kenyas-independence-fight

were the people who knew about him; unfortunately, most of them now have passed away. But in Kenya, I don't fully know why this history hasn't been fully passed down generationally.

GS: Maybe we can build on this a little bit. Is there anything else more broadly that you think is preventing knowledge of your father coming out a bit more?

IG: I think a big part of it was because he was a communist who stood for a type of communism that I would call pristine communism. Communism wasn't just a word for him, the socialist ideologies were ingrained in him by Sikh scriptures and history and Marxist readings. I remember when my mum used to ask him why he was reluctant to join us when we went to the gurdwara and his reply was always that while people just recite the words, he practised the Sikh teachings in his daily life. At his core, he was a humanitarian who cared about the poor and the downtrodden and educated himself about their plight and solutions.

GS: The wider geo-political context of the time is important here, too, as I learnt while working on the Pinto piece. I was consistently told by my interviewees not to forget the time in which Pinto was alive and politically active -- this was the 1950s and the Cold War era was under way.

IG: That is certainly one of the reasons I think that nothing much is said about him today, and I think this erasure is intentional, purposeful. Communism wasn't just a concept to him. He practised what he preached and the West was threatened by those who stood firm on their ideology like this. Communism today is a very watered down version, while my dad's version of communism doesn't fit into today's material-orientated world, one that is focused much more on the individual than society as a whole.

GS: You have spoken about how your dad's commitment to his ideology came before everything else, including his family. And I'm very curious about your mother's role because I think women's roles in these struggles, as the ones who preserve and protect the home life, play a central role yet their story is even further invisibilised. It's something I found with Pinto, too, and the role of his wife Emma.

IG: I remember once when my parents were in a shop together and the shop owner who was an Englishman said to my father, "Mr Singh, do you know that you've got a diamond standing next to you there?" referring to my mother.

GS: And what did your dad say?

IG: Well knowing him, he probably just smiled. Those were backward times that we were living in back then and mum spent many years alone while dad was in prison. During this time, she was ever so careful, never went anywhere by herself, and was always accompanied by my auntie or another relative. Sitting and reflecting on her life, it must have been very tough. She inevitably was uneducated and wasn't politically involved in anything. But she kept her own integrity and that of her family. She did a great job looking after us, even after dad passed away in the 1970s, and hats off to her for it. I think it would be nice to see her role acknowledged more in this.

GS: You also wrote about your dad being quite progressive when it came to gender roles and I found that really interesting because this was a period where women and girls were, as you described it, as a backward society, and so your dad seems to stand out as someone who believed in equality along the lines of gender as well as race.

IG: Yes, he was very committed to that. Soon after he got married, he told my mum that she didn't need to cover her face in front of her father-in-law and other older men as used to be the tradition at the time. This was again an influence from the Guru Granth Sahib. In those days, marriages were arranged, and the bride's friends and aunties would want to test how good the bridegroom's communication skills were. My father included lines from Gurbani in the couplet he recited, which was: "sachai maarag chaladhiaa ousthath karae jehaan" which means 'those who walk on the Path of Truth shall be praised throughout the world'.

His approach benefited me, too, he was very much keen on my getting a PhD after I completed the master's degree in Canada. I got the opportunity to do so after my marriage and it was tough because I had two young children and I had to write the thesis during the early hours of the day. He had passed away by then and while writing I remember talking to him that he wanted me to do this, so please support me.

GS: One writer put your dad into the same bracket as Gandhi, Mandela and Kenyatta for his fight against indifference and segregation. What do you think his legacy is and why does it still matter today?

IG: His legacy is that he set up the trade unions. There were lots of things happening at the time but many groups were not working together or were against each other but he brought together people from different races and was inspired by labour movements in India, which were very well organised. So his legacy, I would say, isn't just that he set up Kenya's first trade union, it was also in Uganda and Tanzania, I would say he is the father of trade unionism in East Africa. Also it was him who sowed the seed of independence of Kenya when in his famous speech he quite categorically said "Uhuru Sasa".

GS: You also wrote that he has left behind a priceless legacy, and a history that inspires and guides us and the coming generations as well. What would you like those in my generation and those who follow to take from his history, from his legacy, from his values?

IG: There's a word in Punjabi called Nishkaam, which means don't have any gain for your own self. And this was the value that my father worked from. He was a humanitarian, always looking to the downtrodden and knew himself what poverty was like because when he was in India, the family was very, very poor. He did that. And he did that wholeheartedly. He fought for equality, which I think in this time and age we need most. It wasn't just race, religion or colour; it was for gender equality, too.

"Finally, then, I just want to end on what would you like to see going forward around the memorialisation of your father's legacy? What can those among us from the generations that have followed do to honour and learn from important figures in our history like your father?"

IG: I think that the best thing to do is bring out the true facts and personal qualities about people like my father and all those who were involved with the independence struggle. Many of those from older generations have shut themselves off from this history but it needs to be brought out. Bringing out the truth of this history and the people who were part of it is the way forward.

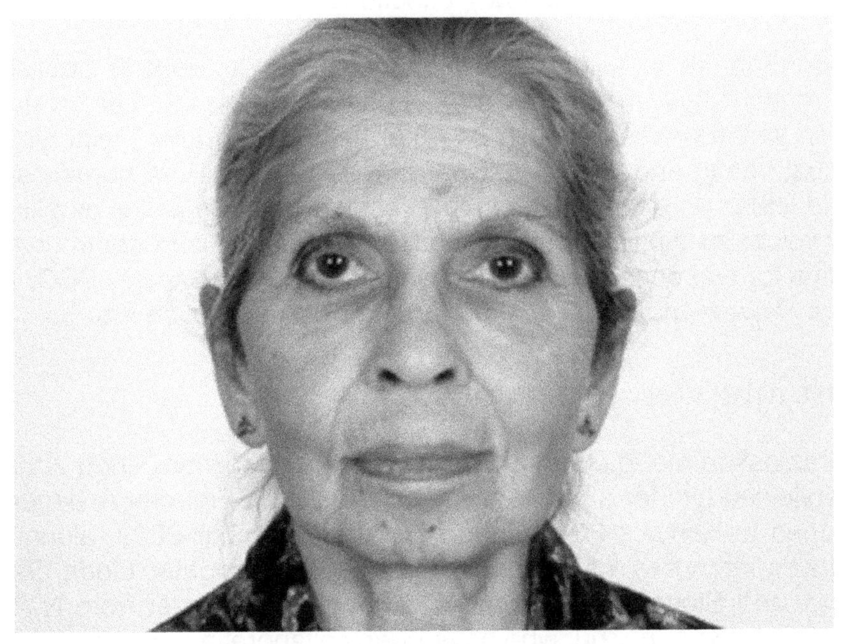

Inderjit Gill Jabbal, the daughter of Makhan Singh.

Gouri Sharma.

Gouri Sharma: Post Interview Reflections

Gouri Sharma is a journalist and writer whose work is published internationally. With roots in Lahore, London, Punjab, Delhi and Nairobi, Gouri writes on issues such as race, culture, migration, history, and sexual health and wellness. She aims to draw out the human story amid wider political and economic contexts, in particular amplifying the voices of those from marginalized and minoritized communities. Active for two decades, she has written for for Al Jazeera, BBC, *MIT Tech Review* and *South China Morning Post*, among others.

Post-interview reflections

Shiraz asked me to contribute to this book on Makhan Singh after I'd interviewed him for a profile piece on Pio Gama Pinto for Al Jazeera. Pegged to Kenya's 60th Jamhuri Day in December 2023, alongside Shiraz's interview, I had spoken with Pinto's daughter Linda Gama Pinto, and Stoneface Bombaa, a community organizer from Nairobi and journalist April Zhu, who have been collaborating on a fascinating podcast series about Pinto and his enduring legacy.

Working on the article – my first on Kenya – left me with more questions than conclusions on figures like Pinto and the history they embody, so in light of this, Shiraz and I decided that a conversation with Inderjit Kaur Gill, Makhan's only daughter, could make for an interesting contribution to this book. Approaching the piece this way would allow for a look at a different side to Makhan, while also allowing me the freedom to explore his life and legacy from an intergenerational perspective.

My paternal side is Kenyan-Indian, my grandmother was born in Nairobi while my grandfather was among the many Indians who migrated to Kenya from Punjab to work in the railways. They married in Kenya (an announcement of which I found recently while flicking through old editions of the *Colonial Times* newspaper holed up at London's Imperial War Museum) and my aunt, dad and three uncles followed later. My aunt married and moved to the US, while the rest of the family later migrated to London in the mid-1960s, around the time of Kenya's independence. My dad, Neelam, was at the time 15 or 16 years old.

Growing up, we – my cousins and two siblings – would often hear stories from my dad and his brothers at family functions about their time in Kenya. Peaceful and playful, they nostalgically spoke of their days joyfully spent outside in the hot Nairobi heat alongside Mombasa beach trips, with the antics of these four boys often landing them in trouble with their no-nonsense dad. They also recalled the roles of our family members, such as my great-grandfather and grandmother who held prominent positions in education. Through these stories though, I never got a sense of the wider political and racial dynamics of the South Asian-Kenya community that were embedded into the British colonial system. Only through learning about my dad's maternal uncle, the journalist DK Sharda, did I start to connect to the bigger picture. As an aspiring journalist myself, I was inspired by Sharda, a firebrand anti-colonial writer and editor who spoke out against the injustices of British rule. Active from the 1930s, he was later deported by the colonial administration to India, where he died within a few years of his expulsion.

Having been raised in the UK, I've found it interesting how the Kenyan-Indian diaspora community relates to Kenya – the place, our history, and the community that remains there. I've also observed quite a big disconnect within this diaspora with India, with many never having visited – nor seeming to have much interest – in connecting with India and our histories there. Ours is the story of the 'double diaspora' that also doesn't receive much coverage or awareness within the international media space, a gap I sought to fill with the Al Jazeera piece on Pinto.

Talking with Inderjit for the piece has provoked further questions for me, but at the same time has created an opening. Learning about the life of her father through her lens was heartening, and it was inspiring to learn that Makhan's fight for human rights and freedom were actively mirrored in his personal life and in his role as a father and husband. His progressive set of values, in particular around gender equality, stood out further given the times that he lived in, and clearly had a positive impact on Inderjit and her academic success later in life.

Gender and the roles South Asian women have played in Kenya are among the areas that I'm keen to learn more about. As was the case of Pio Gama's wife, Emma Pinto, Makhan's wife Satwant Kaur also played an extremely important role that was being carried out in private as he fought in the public. Without the support of his wife to look after the children and keep their home life stable, would Makhan have been able to pursue his vision the way he did? If there is still so much to be told about some of the most well known figures in our history, including Pinto and Makhan, how many more stories remain untold and unheard? As members of the previous generations pass on, including my dad four years ago, what more can we do to share this knowledge with younger people in the diaspora before this history dies along with those that have come before us? There are still many sides to our stories in Kenya, still so much to understand, especially from where I sit at the cross-section between generations and geographies – when it comes to the values, lessons and even contradictions that form a bridge between those of us who share this history, including myself, Inderjit, Makhan and my father.

I'd like to take this opportunity to thank Inderjit for her openness, Shiraz for the opportunity, and Wangechi for the editorial support.

---

https://www.aljazeera.com/features/2023/12/12/pio-gama-pinto-the-indian journalist-who-joined-kenyas-independence-fight

Submerged Narrative: The Untold Side of Makhan Singh's Story

Kenneth S Ombongi[11]

1. Introduction

This chapter is 'another story' on the trade unionist, anti-colonialist, and impenitent socialist, Makhan Singh. It is 'another story' because many a scholar and general writer, including contributors to this volume, have brought their erudition to bear on the life, times and struggles of Singh. It is interesting, however, to realise that much of what we know about Singh is situated within and, mainly, framed in the narratives of his anti-colonial efforts.[12] But away from delineations embedded in decolonising credentials, the racially bifurcated perspectives of White settlers and the colonial establishment saw Singh as an Indian.[13] Much of the indignity he suffered at the hands of the colonial state was, partially, because of that: his *Indian-ness*. From the very nascent imperial years, British colonialists in Kenya eschewed Indians and what they socially constructed as Kenyan *Indian-ness* – the predilection to compete with minority whites in the affairs of the colony; regular demands of their rightful political position within the colonial polity; and the unbridled unity of purpose with Africans they usually deployed in critical junctures in the clamour for justice and fairness.

---

11 Kenneth S Ombongi is a Senior Lecturer and Chairman of the Department of History & Archaeology, University of Nairobi. He holds a PhD from the University of Cambridge, UK Previously, he served as the Principal/Chief Executive Officer at the Kenya Utalii College, the state-owned first hospitality school in sub-Saharan Africa. He, also, served as the African Regional Vice President for the United Nations World Tourism Organization (UNWTO), Affiliate Members Board. His research interests are on areas of social history of biomedicine in Africa as well as the study of African statecraft and electoral politics.

12 A number of studies highlight the general Indian efforts against colonialism in Kenya, including Makhan Singh's activities. See Mangat (1969); Nazareth (1981); Patel (2006); and Seidenberg (1979).

13 The use of the term Indian, in the context of East Africa, is controversial. This is especially after the partition of colonial India into today's India Pakistan and East Pakistan (Bangladesh). The terms Asians and African Asians are generally used nowadays. I confine myself to the original term Indian to refer to people who trace their descent to South Asia to avoid getting into debates of the India-Pakistan binary, which is not relevant to the current subject.

Many of the extant writers on Singh and Indian anti-colonial struggles scarcely acknowledge that there was a way in which all the foregoing realities, which looked like Indian 'excesses' to the colonial authority, provided the bedrock that attracted the state's wrath against Singh's leadership as well as calls for justice and freedom for all. His ability to politically organise and mobilise clearly fitted within the colonial framing and labelling of what they hated Indians for. This chapter is an attempt to bring forth this 'other' story of Makhan Singh. It is divided into five sections. Section One delineates the prelude to the chapter; Section Two outlines the gist of the chapter's argument; Section Three situates Makhan Singh within the colonial notions of the control of Indians while Section Four demonstrates how Singh's efforts in Afro-Indian unity were seen as dangerous to the colonial project and, therefore, totally unwelcome by the colonial authorities. We draw some conclusions in the final section.

2. Argument

As alluded to earlier, much of the contemporary historical articulations, not least understanding, frame the disposition and work of Makhan Singh within the critical but near-conventional trajectory of freedom struggle.[14] The consequent narratives fit into the familiar conceptions of the overly nationalist binary thinking of liberal and non-liberal 'official' histories as well as the socialist and relativist representations of Kenya's anti-colonial insurgency.[15] However, what is important is that the extant delineation of Singh's anti-colonial portrait offers a glimpse into a firebrand socialist and an internationalist working class leader. Cumulatively, besides acknowledging Singh's brazen role in the critical time of decolonising Africa, this approach assuages the regular bemoaning of the excesses of *Afro-centricity* in Kenya's anti-colonial historiography.

However, despite this honoured place in Kenya's historiography, Singh's story has a trajectory which represents a double tragedy of sorts. This facet bespeaks of prevalent dismal appreciation of his leadership role let alone a lifelong dedication to the cause of freedom from colonialism. He was detained in the mop-up of the Mau Mau insurgents in 1950. He remained desolate, but unrepentant, in prison for over 11 years and, that way, became the longest serving prominent Mau Mau detainee.[16] The second side of his double tragedy was that,

14 Patel (2006).

15 Elkins (2005); Anderson (2005); Kinyatti (1991); Munene (2022), Lonsdale (2001)

16 Rattansi (2022).

Singh was not only punished by the British authority in much of the colonial era but was also banished from playing any meaningful role in independent Kenya by his 'fellow' African compatriots. Indeed, he was distrusted by both isms dominant in colonial and post-colonial Kenya. Singh was neither welcome to European imperialism nor African nationalism. It is not hard to infer that the current teleological notions postulate that Singh's travails and tribulations, which threatened to reduce him to a mere footnote in the country's political history, derived from his ultra-radical and socialist working class leadership. In this view, things became worse because his anti-colonial activities happened at a time when the dominant global West (capitalist America and its allies) eschewed any traces of socialist inclinations of the global East (socialist Russia and its allies). This was particularly critical in the immediate independent Kenya, which held the promise of a capitalist bastion in a strongly divided East-West ideological contemporary setting.[17]

It is understandable that the current narratives emphasise Singh's role in Kenya's freedom struggle. Definitely, this overly nationalist view is important. First, it broadens our understanding of a critical vista of a complex life. Second, it affords room for a much maligned local Indian community to bolster a sense of belonging by positively staking claim to the country's history formation and development. However, we argue in this chapter that, in and by themselves, such literatures seldom provide a full picture of the broader socio-political environment that not only fashioned Singh's life but also the corresponding responses to his actions from both the colonial and immediate post-colonial state. We posit that a focus on the circumstances contingent to the wider Kenyan society and the long-drawn development of the racialist ideology of colonial modernity becomes necessary to unravel these muted, not least, submerged dimensions of Singh's struggles. This broad view throws up new light in the much needed *longue duree* stimuli that were important in Singh's world.

In this chapter, we analyse factors and situations that catalysed, in the long term, hostility towards Singh. These included the historical clash of Anglo-Indian interests in Kenya, the racist development policy which fostered a segregated society and the British eschewing of Afro-Indian unity at any one time in the history of the country. It is important to note that this approach historicises Singh into the complex matrix of the social and political world of Kenyan Indians and the dramatic

17 Norworjee (2014).

historical dilemmas they have grappled with over the years in their land of domicile. This will augment ideas of the fairly narrow lenses of anti-colonial-struggle-approach that are enough but insufficient to cover the whole corpus of Singh's life and work in Kenya.

3. Makhan Singh and Shackles of Indo-phobia

The end of the 1950s decade was a period of enormous excitement and endless possibilities for diverse social and racial aggregates in Kenya. For the white settlers, the impending end of the empire, locally, spelt uncertainty and irrelevance of their racial supremacism, which they had clung on for over 70 years of British rule. For the Africans, the period was, glaringly, wrought by the triumph of nationalism, if not the promise of African majority rule with possibilities galore of righting the ills of the bastardised colonial past. However, one group – Indians -- was not very lucky! The dilemmas of the binaries of either belonging or not, citizens or not, safe or not, confronted them, perhaps, much more seriously than in the preceding era.[18] This state of affairs was not new among the Indians in Kenya. It was fashioned and hitherto embedded within a colonial tradition. In this practice, the growth of Indian strategic leadership, not least activities, was nefariously inhibited, controlled and, at times, like in the case of Makhan Singh, outrightly ostracised.

Indians have been at crossroads throughout modern Kenya's history. In pre-colonial Kenya, they confined their commercial activities to the East African littoral, with occasional, albeit treacherous travel to the, largely, unreached hinterland. In the coast, they were a critical cog in the Indian Ocean intercontinental commercial networks in which interests of Africa, Asia, Middle East and Europe intersected. Despite their indispensable commercial role in the Indian Ocean commerce, their significance in the coast was persistently eclipsed by the Arabs since the former seldom established neither permanent settlements nor bases in the region.[19] This was the case, especially from the 7th century onwards, with the spread of Islam and the attendant emergence of the Swahili civilization in which the Afro-Arabic influence was overemphasized; overemphasized, usually, at the expense of Indians' contribution.[20]

The situation, with regard to the position of Indians, was not very different during the British colonial era in Kenya in the twentieth century. While the Indian ambidexterity in the distributive and retail

18 Mangat (1969).

19 Mangat (1969), p1.

20 Mangat (1969)

sectors midwifed the colonial cash economy from the very beginning, their dominance, political or otherwise, was eschewed and fiercely resisted by the British. A colonial narrative that strongly entrenched racial segregation sought to cut Indians to size and confined them to the fringes of society, only better than the majority Africans, who were, basically, in this 'watertight' social system "hewers of wood and drawers of water", to use that biblical phrase.

In Kenya's post-colony, the same fate of Indo-phobia and dilemma befell Indians. Increasingly, they became scapegoats to be chastised for the failures of the embryonic African state.[21] Even worse, revisionist narratives relegated Indians to the echelons of second class citizens without appreciating their role as part of the vanguards of Kenya's freedom struggle. More than any other personality, the story of Makhan Singh illustrates this glaring but unfortunate situation.

India's colonial Gujranwala District, in today's West Pakistan, witnessed Makhan Singh's birth in December 1913; Nairobi, Kenya's colonial capital, gave him an education and an early career in his father's printing press. It, also, launched him into the explosive politics of working class trade unionism and, consequently, he pursued labour movement leadership much of his life.[22]

4. Makhan Singh and Indo-African Alliance

Singh started his trade union career as a representative of the Indian workers, mainly on the Uganda Railway. It all started in 1935, at the young age of 22, when he was elected the General Secretary of the Indian Trade Union (ITU). ITU quickly metamorphosed into the much racially encompassing Labour Trade Union of Kenya (LTUK). By July 1939, LTUK had attracted prominent African unionists, such as Jesse Kariuki and George Ndegwa, who were elected as the union's Vice President and member of the Executive Committee, respectively. By the start of the Second World War, the government dislike for the embryonic Indo-African unity in the workers movement was obvious, especially what Singh described as "the shoulder-to-shoulder struggle of African and Asian workers."[23]

If the foregoing was not enough, Singh got involved, and rather radically so, in the affairs of the East African Indian Congress and

21 Himbara (1994).

22 Nowrojee (2015), pp.18 -20.

23 Nowrojee (2015), p.21.

became a stronger member of its Youth League. Therefore, the colonial authorities sought to silence him before he could get out of control. As a result, he was arrested in 1940 while on a political working trip to India, only to be released in 1945.[24] After his release, Singh hastily returned to Kenya to the chagrin of the colonial state. He intensified his radical approach to trade unionism and fostering an Indo-African front against the ills of colonialism. In 1949, Makhan Singh, with African and Asian trade unionists, organised the East African Trade Unions Congress (EATUC), a central organisation of regional trade unions. It coordinated activities of trade unions in East Africa. Fred Kubai, an African leader, became EATUC's President while Singh became its Secretary General.[25]

In the face of the incessant intensity of political-cum-trade-union activities, a panicky colonial state arrested Singh in 1950 on trumped-up charges. Despite lack of cogent evidence to sustain claims of Singh being a saboteur of good public order, he was detained for 11 years. Makhan Singh's period in detention took him away from the public but did not take away his spirit of rebellion against the colonial state. Even when he was released in 1961, he remained an unrepentant communist, and worked closely with professed African communists such Oginga Odinga and Fred Kubai. Never mind that the colonial government released Singh in 1961 because they thought he had been away long enough "to disrupt every effort at moderation."[26]

However, away from the official rationalisation of Singh's release, the underlying reason for its timing was clear from official circles. In 1961, on the verge of Kenya's independence, with a viable possibility of an African majority rule by the allies of the colonialists, Singh, despite his considerable "influence and organising ability", had no place in the emerging dispensation.[27] In one of the cabinet confidential write-ups then, the government stated its real intention of why Singh had set to be released: "in the circumstances of Kenya today, it is unlikely that a non-African, however fanatical, would emerge as a leader capable of stirring up the African masses."[28] Singh had to be free because he was not a danger any longer. His ability and opportunity to stir up political activity among Africans had dropped dramatically in the view of the

24 Nowrojee (2015), pp.22 - 24.
25 Nowrojee, (2015), p.26.
26 Nowrojee (2015), pp.35 – 36.
27 Nowrojee (2015), p.39
28 Nowrojee (2015), pp.35 – 36.

colonial government.
The fate that befell Singh in the 1950s was, clearly, part of the wider colonial script. It was clear, from the early twentieth century, that colonial authorities, no less the White settlers in Kenya, were determined to checkmate Indian political and economic influence. Initial ideas of a colonial setting dominated by Indians as 'handmaids' of imperial policy was shelved; it was replaced by hostility driven, largely, by the fear of Indians, Indo-phobia. Indo-phobia, besides the need to control Indians to play second fiddle in the colonial racial hierarchy, was constructed around a potential danger of a combined Afro-Indian effort to oppose the colonial state.[29]

Therefore, much earlier before Makhan Singh rose to prominence in Kenya's political scene, any Indian leader who showed any slight signs of political organisation and mobilisation was met with the wrath of the Kenya authorities, there and then. There was a demonstrable historical pattern of the standard fate such leaders met at the hands of government. For example, in the early 1920s one of the emerging African leaders was Harry Thuku, a post office worker, plunged himself into protest politics. In June 1921, Thuku founded the Young Kikuyu Association (YKA), whose main demands on the government included calls to end the discriminative Kipande (identification plate) system for Africans, increased African access to education opportunities and lowering of taxes, among others.[30] Thuku was a close ally and friend of Ambalal Manilal Desai, the leader of the East African Indian Congress who had been in Kenya since 1915. Thuku and Desai shared an office. As a result, Thuku had unfettered access to Desai's printer, a rare technology among Africans then, for publishing political awareness-raising material. In 1922, when Thuku was arrested and a crowd demanding his release at the Central Police Station in downtown Nairobi was violently dispersed, Desai became a marked man by the colonial security agents. From then, henceforth, until he died in 1926, he remained tacit, if not discreet, in his Indo-African political operations.[31] By the 1950s, when Makhan Singh was writ large in working class anti-government political activities, another

29 In the last decade of the 19th century, during the initial days of the establishment of British East Africa as Kenya was called then, there were official notions galore that saw Indians as a critical group in 'opening up' East Africa for 'civilization'. In some official circles East Africa was envisaged "as a possible America of the Hindu." Mangat (1969), p.64

30 Ochieng' (1985), pp.117 – 118.

31 Seidenberg (1979)

Indian publisher, editor of the *Colonial Times,* Girdhalal Vidyarthi, had his career cut short for his inclination to support the African cause.[32]

It is no wonder that Makhan Singh would meet the same fate. Throughout his life and career, he challenged the colonial models of *Indian-ness*, what Indians were to be and do locally. He refused to fit within the narrow identity and racist paradigms of separate development and segregation. Accounts of Singh's close associates, those who knew and worked with him, reveal a diehard character and non-conformist.[33] He favoured Indo-African unity against the colonial oppressive labour laws to the chagrin of European administrators. Throughout the period, from the 1930s to 1960s, of his militant trade union career, he refused to be confined into the prevalent Eurocentric notions of how local Indians ought to behave politically. For operating outside the colonial ideals of Indian conduct, Makhan Singh suffered harassment; he lived perpetually under the threat of deportation to India, if not thrown into the detention as it happened first between 1939 and 1945 in India and 1950 to 1961 in Kenya. Just like his previous compatriots, Makhan Singh had to be separated from politically 'contaminating' Africans. In the run-up to Kenya's independence, while the British were willing to negotiate a settlement with Jomo Kenyatta, a political detainee just like Singh, they wanted Singh out of public life for good. If Kenyatta was a lesser evil to be tolerated, Singh was regarded as a monster to be banished from public life. This was basically in the nature of colonialism and its relations with Indians throughout the colonial era.[34] It is axiomatic, therefore, that Singh not only infuriated but also demonstrated a formidable predilection to disturbing *Pax Britannica* in Kenya.[35] This was so much so that the clarion call that 'Makhan Singh must go' could have aptly described British intentions, not least reactions, against his gallant actions. He was viewed as a trouble-maker and instigator!

The irony was that the post-colonial regime, despite being borne of the demands for fairness and justice, did the same thing to Singh as its colonial predecessor. He was never allowed to play any meaningful political role in Kenya's post-colony life by his Africa comrades in the struggle for freedom. Other prominent Indians, too, had to contend with a similar dilemma as Singh's. It was as if the old Indo-phobia found its

32 Ombongi (1993)

33 Rattansi (2022), p.8.

34 Rattansi (2022), p.8.

35 Rattansi (2022), p.10.

'rightful' place in independent Kenya's polity. A few of those Indians who defied this colonial carry-over of Indo-phobia to independent Kenya could not withstand the discriminative elite African nationalism. For example, Pio Gama Pinto, an Indian of Goan origin and a professed socialist, met his premature death in 1965 at a young age in what appeared as a politically-motivated assassination. Ambubhai Patel, a man who had put his printing skills at the disposal of the African champions of the freedom struggle, like AM Desai before him, felt that Pinto's fate might befall him. He hurriedly left Kenya for good. It was unfortunate that Ambubhai Patel did not stay longer in independent Kenya to make available his rich collection of documentary source material to yield useful insights in rewriting the history of Kenya, especially the intrigues of the years leading up to independence.

5. Conclusion

In this chapter, we have made an attempt at a biographical analysis of Makhan Singh. The fundamental goal of the chapter was to establish a locale for this vibrant working class leader in order to historicise his important role within the wider and complex labyrinth of Kenya's imperial arena with, largely, volatile race relations and inherent hierarchies of power in an African setting. The colonially imposed three-tier racial order in Kenya demanded nothing but Indian subservience and separate development from that of Africans. Often, at critical junctures throughout the colonial era, dissent against such structural inequalities threw up brave Indian leadership that championed Afro-Indian militant protest against the colonial state. This situation fostered some form of Indo-phobia among the White settlers and government officials. It happened in such ways that popularised ideals of keeping Indians and Africans politically separated. Any violations of these widely held notions of 'separate development', as formulated and executed by the White minority, met with either open or tacit, but extreme, arm-twisting frustrations or mistreatment from the colonial authorities. Makhan Singh was a perennial victim of this unfortunate situation. This was so either when he was in India or Kenya. Such hostile official treatment did not only culminate in his detention in 1950 and several, albeit vain, attempts to either jail or deport him. Earlier, in the 1920s, in like manner, his compatriot, AM Desai, equally ran into headwinds with the colonial authorities for the same reasons as Singh did. The celebrated printers, Ambu Patel and Girdhalal Vidyarthi, would suffer the same fate in the late 1940s and 50s.[36]

---

36 Ombongi (1993).

Clearly, therefore, Singh was an embodiment of Kenya's chequered colonial past; a boundless fighter for freedom and justice, a professed communist, and a trade unionist par excellence whose life served as a salutary example of the suffering of those who choose sacrifice over abundance and service over self for the larger good of society.

References

Ghai, Dharam, P (1965), Portrait of a Minority, Nairobi, Oxford University Press.

Gregory, R (1971 a), India and East Africa: A History of Race Relations with the British Empire 1890-1939. London: Oxford University Press.

Gregory, R (1971 b), South Asians in East Africa: An Economic and Social History. Boulder Colorado: West View Press.

Hilmer, J (2008), The State of Participatory Democratic Theory. A Paper Presented at the 66 Annual Meeting of the Mid West Political Science Association. April3 -- 6, 2008, Chicago, USA.

Himbara, D (1994), Kenya Capitalists, the State and Development. Nairobi: EAE Publishers.

Hollingsworth, LW (1960), The Asians of East Africa, London.

Mangat, JS (1969), A History of Asians in East Africa, 1886 to 1945, Oxford: Clarendon Press.

Nabende, J (1996), 'The Political Economy of Education for Asians in Kenya' in Kiriama Herman (1996). The Asian Question in Kenya. The Eastern Africa Journal of Historical and Social Sciences Research, Vol.1, No.1.

Nazareth, J (1981), Brown Man, Black Country: A Peep into Kenya's Freedom Struggle. New Delhi: Tiding Publications.

Ngari, L (1996), The Indian Question. The East African Journal of Historical and Social Sciences Research Vol.1. No.1.

Nowrojee, P (2007), Pio Gama Pinto: Patriot for Social Justice. Nairobi: Sasa Publications.

Nowrojee, Pheroze (2014), A Kenyan Journey, Nairobi, Transafrica Press.

Ochieng, W (1980), Makhan Singh (1952-1956): Crucial years of Kenya Union of Trade Congress. Nairobi: Uzima Press Ltd.

Odinga, O (1966), Pio Gama Pinto: Kenya's First Political Martyr. Nairobi: New Africa Press.

Ombongi, K (1993), Hindu Socio-Religious Organizations in Kenya: A Case Study of Arya Samaj, 1903-1978. MA Thesis, University of

Nairobi.
Patel, Zarina (1997), Challenge to Colonialism: The struggle of Alibhai Mulla Jeevanjee, Nairobi, Zand Press.
Patel, Zarina (2006), Unquiet: The life and times of Makhan Singh, Nairobi, Kenya Human Rights Commission.
Seidenberg, A (1983), 'Asians and Uhuru. The Role of a Minority Community in Kenyan Politics, 1939-1963.' A PhD Thesis, Syracuse University.
Thuku, H (1970) (with Kenneth King), Story of my life, Nairobi, Oxford University Press.

The Footprints of Makhan Singh in Kenya's Working Class Struggles and National Liberation

Oduor Ong'wen[37]

Introduction

This article delves into the profound impact of Makhan Singh's defining role within Kenya's working-class struggles and the broader context of national liberation. Singh's legacy is entwined with the inception of worker organisation amid colonial and settler exploitation. The narrative traces the evolution from what were seen as sporadic protests to the establishment of unions, embodying a transformative journey fraught with challenges — economic exploitation, racial bias, and colonial dominance.

The resistance against colonial rule commenced with peasant-led uprisings, progressively transitioning to organised labour-driven movements. Strikes, resistance along the Uganda Railway, armed clashes, and mobilisation by figures like Waiyaki wa Hinga and Ngunyu wa Gakeere exemplify the diverse efforts against colonial occupation. The labour movements not only challenged economic exploitation but also sought equitable treatment, housing, and fair wages.

Singh emerges as a pivotal figure shaping Kenya's struggle for independence. His leadership within trade unions, alongside working class leaders like Chege Kibacia, Bildad Kaggia and Fred Kubai, contributed to the radicalisation of the workers' movement. These unions became instrumental in articulating workers' demands and

37 Oduor Ong'wen holds a B.Sc degree in Statistics & Operations Research and an MA in Economics. He is currently pursuing an M.Sc. in Global Management (June 2024). He is Executive Director of the Orange Democratic Movement, where his leadership contributes to shaping policies and strategies within the political landscape. He previously was Country Director at the Southern and Eastern Africa Trade Information and Negotiations Institute (SEATINI), where he played a pivotal role in trade dynamics and negotiations across the region. He also served as the Executive Director of EcoNews Africa, fostering sustainable development initiatives and environmental advocacy. He has authored many scholarly and popular press articles and two books – Oduor Ong'wen & Nishu Aggarwal (eds). *Towards A Working Agenda: Report on NGO/African Development Bank Consultations*, African Development Bank, Abidjan 1994 and Oduor Ong'wen, *Stronger than Faith: My Journey in the Quest for Justice in Kenya 1958-2015*, Vita Books, Nairobi, 2022.

engaging in larger political battles against colonial oppression.

However, the post-independence era unfolded in a manner incongruent with the aspirations of Makhan Singh and his comrades. The rise of a new elite, failure in fostering a distinct counter-culture, and alignment with mainstream nationalist formations contributed to an outcome that fell short of the envisioned transformative change.

Singh's legacy highlights the importance of unity across oppressed classes, autonomous union movements, grassroots empowerment, and international solidarity. His narrative illustrates the need for a cohesive counter-culture advocating radical change, transcending the limitations of a two-stage liberation mindset.

The evolution of worker organisation in Kenya represent a pivotal facet of the country's historical narrative. Rooted in the intersection of economic exploitation, colonial imposition, and the quest for equitable treatment, the genesis of organised labour movements predates Kenya's official colonial status.

Kenya's history intertwines tightly with the burgeoning workers' struggles, marked by the first documented strike in 1900 (Durrani, 2009). This crucial moment aligned with the influx of foreign capital introduced through the Imperial British East Africa Company and the establishment of the Kenya-Uganda railway. These developments were targeted to streamline the extraction and exportation of raw materials as well as the importation of manufactured goods, setting the stage for the labour tensions that would ensue. Crucially, the genesis of worker resistance remained interlinked with the broader anti-colonial resistance. Employers, predominantly settlers and colonial government figures, who were often foreigners themselves, perpetuating the autocratic trends of the colonial regime. As Mohamed (2021) asserts, the initial workers' strikes manifested as spontaneous acts, frequently marked by violence and disruption. These early eruptions in the transport sector, notably at ports and railways, served as the rudimentary stirrings of collective action preceding formal unionisation.

The formal declaration of Kenya as a British colony in 1920 marked a nodal juncture in the labour movement's trajectory. Until then, workers were segregated along racial and ethnic lines – European, Indian, and African labourers, with further divisions among African workers being looked at as Gikuyu, Luo, Kamba, Luyia, among others. Such stratification not only reflected the colonial administration's divisive tactics but also underscored the complexities within the labour struggles.

The journey towards organised labour in Kenya was arduous, reflecting a mosaic of challenges that included not just economic exploitation but also deeply ingrained racial and ethnic divisions. These divisions were deliberately fostered by the colonial powers to prevent unified dissent against their exploitative practices. Furthermore, the evolution of the labour movement in Kenya highlights a critical progression from sporadic, unorganised protests to the eventual formation of unions. The initial "spontaneous" strikes, primarily in the transportation sector, were foundational to the subsequent structuring of organised labour movement. These unions became central in articulating the demands of the workers and negotiating better working conditions, fair wages, and overall improved treatment within the colonial economic framework.

In essence, the roots of organised labour in Kenya can be traced back to the dawn of colonial economic exploitation. The progression from what were derisively labelled sporadic protests to the establishment of unions represents a transformative journey, reflective of the resilience and determination of workers to assert their rights on a landscape characterised by foreign capital, colonial oppression, and deep-seated racial divisions.

Peasants Cede the Vanguard of Resistance to Workers

The initial resistance against colonial rule in Kenya was peasant-led and lacked a national approach even if it spanned geographical boundaries and encompassed various ethnic groups and communities. It was a concerted effort driven by grievances over land annexation, forced labour, taxation, cultural oppression, and other forms of colonial exploitation and control. This resistance was not limited to a singular community or region; rather, it evolved into a widespread movement encompassing various nationalist uprisings, localised worker resistance movements, and armed engagements against British colonial forces.

The first resistance against British occupation in Kenya was marked by the uprising of Kenyan coastal peoples under the leadership of Mbaruk Al Amin Mazrui between 1895 and 1896. Their guerrilla warfare posed a significant challenge to the British, compelling the latter to deploy a special task force from India to suppress the revolt (Ong'wen, 2022). Simultaneously, the construction of the Uganda Railway faced significant delays due to resistance from Kenyan peasants and indentured workers from the Indian subcontinent. Strikes, go-slows, and protests by these workers disrupted progress and led to confrontations with British supervisors.

The construction of the railway presented a focal point for resistance along its route and at administrative posts. Armed clashes between patriotic peasant forces and British colonial occupiers were frequent, with the colonialists relying on mercenaries from India and Sudan to quell the resistance. In central Kenya, the resistance against the Imperial British East Africa Company was led by figures like Waiyaki wa Hinga and Ngunyu wa Gakeere, whose military organisation and leadership posed a formidable challenge to British troops. The resistance in this region persisted until the capture of Waiyaki, whose subsequent being buried alive epitomised the brutality faced by those resisting colonial rule.

Further along the railway route, the Nandi patriots, led by Koitalel arap Samoei, engaged in a decade-long guerrilla campaign against the British between 1895 and 1905. Despite securing major victories, they were eventually overcome by the better-armed colonial forces, marking another chapter in the struggle against occupation (Durrani, 2009).

The resistance efforts extended beyond armed confrontations. The labour movements also played a leading role in challenging colonial exploitation. The Labour Trade Union of Kenya, in its Second Annual General Meeting in September 1936, advocated an eight-hour workday. After a 62-day strike, which ended on June 3, 1937, the workers achieved success with employers in Nairobi agreeing to the demand for an eight-hour workday, wage increases ranging from 15 to 22 per cent, and recognition of workers' rights to union representation (Zeleza, 1993; Durrani, 2009).

Moreover, strikes led by dock and railway workers in Dar es Salaam, Mombasa, Nairobi, and Zanzibar during the 1940s, as noted by Oberst (1988), underscored the widespread nature of dissent against colonial exploitation, which was not confined to Kenya. The interconnection between these cities along the Indian Ocean coast, their economic significance, and their roles as hubs of colonial administration and revenue collection fostered solidarity and facilitated the spread of resistance movements. The geographical spread of these strikes and their timing across multiple cities underscored the interconnectedness of grievances among workers and the impact of communication networks in catalysing coordinated resistance. This further emphasises the significance of solidarity among diverse communities in their collective struggle against colonial oppression.

Trade Unions, Mau Mau and the Struggle for Independence

The genesis and foundation of the Kenya Land Freedom Army (KFLA), popularly known as Mau Mau Independence Movement, have not been adequately recognised, particularly in regard to the role of the working class. The struggle of the Mau Mau, coupled with the independent trade union movement, significantly influenced Kenya's trajectory toward independence. These were not isolated movements but interlinked aspects of a larger drive against British imperialism, advocating self-governance, social equity, and economic autonomy. Individuals like Dedan Kimathi, along with countless unnamed heroes who took up arms against colonial rule and settler dominance, guided the masses – workers, peasants, urban impoverished, and the unemployed. These groups, steered by a strong anti-imperialist ideology, secured a momentous triumph over colonialism, cementing the enduring spirit of independence and sovereignty.

Trade unions, spearheaded by figures like Makhan Singh, Chege Kibacia, Fred Kubai, and Bildad Kaggia, played a critical role in organising workers, later forming the militant forces of KFLA. The trade unions furnished Mau Mau with a revolutionary agenda, propelling one of the most significant and radical wars against the British Empire. Stemming from the radical segments of the Kenya African Union (KAU), led by Kubai and Kaggia, both of whom were rooted in the radical trade union movement, they grew disillusioned with the belief that negotiation with the British would grant Kenya its independence.

Within urban landscapes and White settler domains, worker consciousness burgeoned, giving rise to militant worker organisations such as the Labour Trade Union of Kenya, African Workers Federation (AWF), and the East African Trade Union Congress. (EATUC) This environment fostered prominent working-class and national political leaders like Makhan Singh, Chege Kibacia, Shah Mohammed, Mwangi Macharia, and Fred Kubai. The incipient organisation of Kenya's working class highlighted their class steadfastness, determination, and vanguard role in pursuing social justice in contemporary times. They comprehended that without their labour, settler plantations would yield naught, factories would lie dormant, transportation would cease, and towns would morph into desolate ghettos. Leveraging strikes, boycotts, picketing, and at times sabotage, workers induced political crises, propelling the nationalist anti-colonial struggle.

The initial significant strike emerged in Mombasa in 1939, followed by a 12-day General Strike in 1947 orchestrated by the African Workers Federation, led by Chege Kibacia. The issues encompassed poor housing, paltry wages, racial bias, and police oppression, among other longstanding grievances of Mombasa's labour force. Over 15,000 workers participated, and were met by the colonial government's coercive retaliation. Deploying armed forces and imposing a news blackout, the authorities arrested more than 500 workers, compelling the closure of schools and bombarding the island with leaflets from Royal Air Force planes urging worker surrender. In August 1947, Chege Kibacia was arrested, subjected to a secret trial, and swiftly deported to a remote area, enduring a decade of preventive detention. Eighteen other leaders faced arrest and imprisonment.

Though the arrests and subsequent detention of the majority of the AWF leadership undermined the union's capacity to lead the workers' struggle, it failed to extinguish the spirit of resistance. The East African Trade Union Congress, under Makhan Singh's tireless and revolutionary leadership as General Secretary, assumed responsibility. The union transcended economism, actively engaging workers in major political battles for liberation from colonial shackles. It outpaced KAU in objectives, strategies, and tactics, organising around improving economic, social, and political conditions, safeguarding workers' rights, and advocating freedom of speech, press, association, assembly, and movement. EATUC sought the abolition of discrimination based on race, ethnicity, caste, creed, religion, or sex. Its "Twenty-four Urgent Demands" included an eight-hour workday, minimum wage tied to living costs, enhanced workers' compensation, compulsory employer-funded insurance for unemployment, old age, accidents, and maternity, and abolition of the *kipande* system. Unlike KAU, which adhered to civil political discourse methods, the organised workers of Kenya recognised armed struggle as imperative against British obduracy. Trade unionist Makhan Singh, in 1950, introduced an explicit demand for immediate national independence into KAU's otherwise passive programme. This stance gained support from KAU's most progressive and militant branch in Nairobi, led by radical trade unionists Fred Kubai and Bildad Kaggia, who were chairman and secretary, respectively.

While colonial authorities dismissed peasant revolts as nuisances and contained them effectively, the swelling Kenyan trade union movement, its revolutionary objectives, and the escalating political stature of its radical leadership posed daunting challenges. Workers asserted their power during the May Day Parade of 1950 in Nairobi, captivating tens of thousands with radical speeches and clear demands. Shortly after this rally, on May 15, 1950, EATUC was banned, and its leaders, Makhan Singh and Fred Kubai, were arrested and incarcerated. Makhan Singh, deemed the ideologue and intellectual force behind the trade union movement, endured over a decade behind bars. However, workers weren't intimidated. They swiftly organised a nationwide strike demanding the immediate release of their leaders, a new minimum wage, the end to repressive taxicab bylaws, cessation of arbitrary worker arrests, and total and unconditional national independence for Kenya, Uganda, and Tanganyika. Engaging over 100,000 workers for nine days across Nairobi, Mombasa, Kisumu, Nakuru, and other towns, the strike challenged the colonial economy. Yet, the colonial authorities responded predictably, detaining numerous workers, organisers, and activists for extended periods.

The repressive measures taken by colonial authorities against workers' struggle failed to quell the hunger for freedom; instead, it fuelled a fervent pursuit of liberation. The 1950 General Strike acted as a catalyst for Kenya's liberation struggle. Subsequently, Kenya's workers became more militant and engaged in ongoing national political struggles. During the June 1951 KAU elections, radical trade unionists benefitted from the dividends of clandestine mobilisation, securing leadership positions in the Nairobi branch, and thereafter transformed it into a vibrant force that mobilised, recruited, and funded KAU. Some of these leaders formed the core of the covert Mau Mau Movement. Contrary to the prevalent belief propagated by settler apologists and conservative intellectuals that Mau Mau was a primitive peasant revolt, it was predominantly the militant urban workers in settler plantations who constituted the original, most politically conscious core of the Kenya Land Freedom Army. The vacuum created by the prohibition of workers' organisations, imprisonment of leaders, and KAU's failure to advocate immediate Kenyan demands fueled an intensification in clandestine political organisation. Radical KAU leaders in Nairobi coalesced into an underground group termed the "Forty Group"

(Anake a 40), including Kaggia, Kubai, Isaac Gathanju, and Eliud Mutonyi. This group birthed the Mau Mau Central Committee, the nerve centre of anti-colonial armed struggle. With 12 members, the Central Committee orchestrated a recruitment drive, administering an anti-colonial oath of unity binding members to discipline, secrecy, solidarity, and commitment. Workers' leaders like Kaggia and Kubai were members, although holding no official positions. By 1952, Kenya faced a crisis, witnessing unparalleled restlessness among the downtrodden masses demanding political change. Defiance against colonial authorities became routine, civil disobedience a norm, leaving British colonialists facing an open rebellion.

Makhan Singh's Enduring Influence

The transformation of workers' movements amid colonial and settler exploitation marked a defining era in Kenya's history, reflecting a struggle against worker exploitation and oppressive systems. The dynamics of this evolution, exemplified by Makhan Singh, underscored the imperative of unity against a "divide-and-rule" strategy entrenched by colonial powers. Singh's profound initiatives sought to bridge racial, ethnic, and religious divides among the oppressed classes while advocating resolution of common grievances: meager wages, racial subjugation, and colonial dominance (Patel, 2006).

Singh's approach wasn't solely localised but ideologically rooted in the tenets of international trade unionism. Drawing inspiration from Karl Marx's observations on the symbiotic relationship between capitalism and state intervention, Singh perceived the need for a dual-front struggle. This entailed confronting both capitalist enterprises and the reinforcing arm of the capitalist state, advocating a union movement intrinsically tied to political activism against the bulwark of capitalism (Marx, 1847). Such convictions earned Singh the epithet of a "communist agitator," emphasising his dedication to weaving socialist principles into the fabric of union actions (Olende, 2016).

However, Singh's vision extended beyond ideological orientation. He emphasised the imperative for unions to engage politically while maintaining their autonomy, eschewing subordination to political parties whose ideological orientations were hazy at best. Singh orchestrated broad alliances around specific issues, leveraging union strength for struggles transcending workplace boundaries. Yet, he vehemently opposed excessive entanglement of unions within established systems, often challenging legal norms and fostering defiance when necessary (Van der Walt, 2013).

Central to Singh's philosophy was the empowerment of grassroots union members. He understood that the vitality of unions lay not in a few leaders but in an actively engaged base. This grassroots empowerment served as a safeguard against union degeneration and undue reliance on singular leaders or bureaucratic control. Singh recognised that the true power of unions emanated from a participatory and informed membership base (Van der Walt, 2013).

Furthermore, Singh pioneered international solidarity between Kenyan trade unions and those in other colonies, countering the tendencies of established unions like the British Trade Union Congress (TUC) that aligned with colonial and settler interests. His efforts echoed the observation that imperialism seeped into the working class, blurring the lines between metropolis and peripheries and undermining the basis of international solidarity Emmanuel (1970), Rodney (1972), Samir (2018).

Singh's foresight extended to the necessity of an independent workers' media. Recognising its pivotal role, he leveraged communication mediums — ranging from publications to theatre and broadcasts— to unify and mobilse workers. This enabled the union to articulate its perspectives, circumvent commercial or state media biases, and foster a vibrant print culture (Connoy, 1909).

His overarching vision aimed beyond immediate reforms. Singh, akin to the Ghadar Party, Bakunin, the IWW, and Communists, acknowledged the need for structural societal change. He envisioned unions as pivotal agents in challenging societal divisions, aligning immediate struggles with the broader objective of reshaping society for the benefit of the oppressed classes (Rocker, 1938). His first act in the Labour Trade Union in 1935 was to buy a cyclostyle machine for cheap printing and mass communication. The union disseminated materials in a range of languages and forms, from newsletters to posters to handbills. This allowed the union to speak in its own voice, avoiding reliance on press statements, limiting misrepresentations by the commercial and state media, and provided a means of organising people and while fostering a popular print culture. It enabled the development of a network of contacts, and the dissemination of ideas, proposals and symbols.
This extended struggle necessitated a concerted effort against the

entrenched class system, advocating reforms within the existing system while challenging its inherent inequalities. Singh's aspiration for decolonisation transcended mere power shifts; it encompassed the promotion of national and democratic rights while aspiring for a society liberated from capitalism and class divisions.

Nevertheless, Singh realised that unions, though potent allies, couldn't singularly represent all oppressed groups. Instead, they could serve as crucial allies for broader movements, providing resources, structure, and experience. Singh echoed the IWW's call for internationalism, emphasising the importance of solidarity across borders and industries (Baker, 1923).

In a nutshell, Singh's legacy exemplifies a multifaceted struggle against exploitation and oppression, rooted in fostering unity across diverse oppressed classes, infusing ideological conviction within unionism, maintaining union autonomy, empowering grassroots participation, advocating broader societal change, and embracing international solidarity. His paradigm underscores the potential of unions as agents of change within a larger struggle for social justice and liberation.

Lessons for Kenyan Left

Makhan Singh, a fulcrum personality in Kenya's struggle for independence, witnessed the profound betrayal of national liberation ushering in a system that contradicted the ideals for which he had struggled and suffered. The post-independence era saw the ascendancy of black colonial collaborators and their offspring and an emergent petty bourgeois and comprador elite, yet not the anticipated vanguard of the liberation movement—the working class, the peasantry, and the marginalised. Instead, power transitioned to a new black kleptocracy. Land reforms favoured those tied to colonial collaborators rather than advancing social justice. Exploitation of labour, authoritarian workplaces, and widespread poverty persisted, exacerbating societal divisions. Even the trade unions, once symbols of empowerment, fell prey to transnational economic interests, and lost their autonomy. The defeat of the British Empire was undoubtedly a triumph, but the spoils of victory were disproportionately distributed in favour of the new elite. Makhan Singh's marginalisation paralleled the disillusionment with the larger aspirations he harboured. Analysing this outcome involves acknowledging the intentions of the British imperial state, which sought compliant emergent elites, aligning their interests with a seamless transition to power. However, critiquing this historical turn shouldn't diminish Singh's remarkable contributions. Instead, it's an endeavour to learn from his legacy, examining its limitations to forge a clearer path forward.

One glaring weakness was the failure to construct an alternative, radical counter-culture centred on transformative ideas. Singh, despite his radical inclinations, refrained from publicly advocating his far-Left views or forming a distinct political entity. His acceptance of the KANU manifesto without reservation in the 1960s underscored this. Even colonial government reports acknowledged Singh's reticence in disseminating radical ideas among the populace (Sticher, 1975).

In eschewing the formation of a socialist party, Singh and radical nationalists failed to appreciate a core fundamental observation by Marx, who posited that the initial step involves workers improving their protection from employer demands by uniting through unions. This collective action serves the collective good of all members, not solely limited to solidarity and trust but encompassing a moral stance against the competitive pursuit of profits by capitalists. For socialism to thrive, these principles must expand and serve as its foundational pillars.

Subsequently, political parties provide workers with a platform not just to confront employers but to effect societal change. During Marx's era, socialist-oriented parties existed, raising questions not about unions as the source of such parties, but rather about the dynamics between unions and socialist entities. The socialism advocated by these parties extended beyond the working class, requiring solidarity, trust, and morality to encompass the entire society. Unions relied on socialist parties to challenge capitalism.

As capitalism burgeoned, owners of capital leaned on the state for support in conflicts with workers, prompting workers to engage on dual fronts: against capitalist enterprises and the capitalist state. Success demanded that unions resist state intervention favouring employers. Marx stressed the need for workers to engage in both political and economic struggles. This broadened struggle to aim at societal transformation, not just workplace issues. Marx underscored the necessity for workers' union battles against capitalists to merge into a political fight against the capitalist state, the primary stronghold of capitalism. This shift expanded the struggle, leading to unions aligning with groups advocating for people of color, women, immigrants, and others. A united front rooted in solidarity, trust, and justice sought to transform society comprehensively. If Makhan Singh and his comrades in the trade union movement had internalised this, independent Kenya would have taken a different trajectory. The argument that repression stifled this development doesn't fully hold, considering the survival of local Ghadarites amidst earlier repressions. Moreover, racial dynamics can't singularly account for this failure, as evidenced by strong Left-wing traditions in Mozambique and South Africa. The colonial government's fear of Singh's ideas spreading among the masses emphasised their potential, yet no significant alternative force emerged – especially after Jomo Kenyatta's ruthless suppression and eventual proscription of the Kenya Peoples' Union (KPU). Nationalist formations like Kenya Africa Union and KANU monopolised the political landscape.

Another factor contributing to this outcome was a prevailing tendency within sections of the Left and Communist movements to envision a two-stage struggle for national liberation. This schema prioritised achieving independent statehood led by nationalists in the first stage, deferring the pursuit of socialism to a later phase—a view seemingly aligned with Singh's approach. His collaboration with Kubai in the 1940s and later involvement with Kenyatta and KANU reflected this stance. The allure of a two-stage approach lies in the attainability and popularity of independent statehood as a tangible victory, potentially weakening colonial powers. Historical precedents like Russia, China, and Cuba quickening their transition from the "bourgeois" to "socialist" stages reinforce this perspective. However, in most instances, this approach proves problematic for the Left, often resulting in an overemphasis on supporting nationalists while downplaying ideological differences.

A classic case illustrating this is the South African Communist Party's transformation from a powerful independent force in the 1940s to a subordinate ally of the African National Congress (ANC) by the 1950s. This inclination of the Left to align closely with nationalists hindered the development of a distinct radical platform, limiting the scope for a transformative agenda. In hindsight, the lessons from Makhan Singh's era underscore the importance of crafting a cohesive counter-culture advocating radical change. It necessitates a strategic shift away from a two-stage liberation mindset, ensuring that the pursuit of independent statehood doesn't eclipse the broader socialist aspirations. Building alternative poles of attraction beyond mainstream nationalist formations becomes crucial for genuine transformative change.

Conclusion

The footprints of Makhan Singh within Kenya's working-class struggles and the broader quest for national liberation is undeniably immense, yet immensely under-examined and largely underappreciated. His leadership, alongside other prominent trade unionists and liberation figures, ushered in an era of transformative change rooted in challenging economic exploitation, racial bias (colour bar), and colonial dominance. Singh's journey illuminates the evolution of organised labour in Kenya from scattered protests to the establishment of formidable, nationalist unions. The struggles against colonial rule transitioned from peasant-led resistance to a more organised labour-driven movement. Strikes, armed clashes, and mobilisations led by influential figures exemplified the multifaceted efforts against colonial occupation. Singh emerged as the foremost intellectual force yet unpatronising to his comrades, shaping Kenya's struggle for independence, rallying workers' movements and advocating equitable treatment, fair wages, and grassroots empowerment.

However, the post-independence era did not fulfil the envisioned transformative change. The rise of a new elite, failure to foster a distinct counter-culture, and alignment with mainstream nationalist formations fell short of Singh's aspirations. Yet, his legacy underscores crucial lessons for the Kenyan Left and movements worldwide. Attempts by post-independent political organisations like the December Twelve Movement (DTM) and later MWAKENYA, UWAKE and the Communist Party of Kenya have not succeeded in forging an organic linkage between the mainstream body of the working class and political organisations – the concerted attempts notwithstanding.

This failure to construct a distinct counter-culture advocating a radical change and the adherence to a two-stage liberation mindset hindered the realisation of broader socialist aspirations. Singh's marginalisation post-independence is a caution on the pitfalls of aligning too closely with mainstream nationalist formations, which often diluted the radical platform needed for transformative change.

In essence, Makhan Singh's legacy embodies a fervent call for unity, autonomy, and ideological clarity within the struggle for social justice and liberation. His experiences serve as a prism through which to re-evaluate strategies, emphasising the need for a cohesive counter-culture advocating radical change while remaining wary of compromising ideological integrity for short-term gains.

References

Barker, T 1923. 'The Story of the Sea.' *Chicago: Industrial Workers of the World*, pp. 66-69, 78.

Connolly, J 1909. *Socialism Made Easy.* Chicago: Charles H. Kerr, p. 48.

Durrani, S (2009). 'Trade Union Movement Leads the Way in Kenya.' *Information, Society and Justice, Vol.2 No.2,* 197-204.

Hinden, R 'Socialism and the Colonial World', in Arthur Creech Jones, New Fabian Colonial Essays, The Hagarth Press, London, pp. 9-12 (as cited in Zeleza, op.cit)

Hwang D 2010. 'Korean Anarchism before 1945: A Regional and Transnational Approach.' In Hirsch, S.J. and van der Walt, L. (eds.). *Anarchism and Syndicalism in the Colonial and Post-colonial World, 1870-1940: The Praxis of National Liberation, Internationalism, and Social Revolution.* Brill: Leiden, pp. 95-130.

Marx, K (1847). 'Wage Labour and Capital.' Collected Works, Vol. 42, Progressive Publishers, Moscow.

Mohamed, SR (2021). 'The History of Labour Movement in East Africa: The Case of Kenya and Tanzania.' *International Journal of Research and Innovation in Social Science, Vol.V Issue 2,* 2021.

Oberst, T (1988). 'Transport Workers, Strikes and the —Imperial Responsell: Africa and the Post World War II Conjuncture.' *African Studies Review, Vol. 31, No. 1 (*Apr., 1988), pp. 117-133, Cambridge University Press;

Olende, K (2016). 'Makhan Singh: A revolutionary Kenyan Trade Unionist.' *Socialist Worker, Issue 410* , https://socialistworker.co.uk/socialist-review-archive/makhan-singh-revolutionary-kenyan-trade-unionist/

Ong'wen, O (2022). *Stronger Than Faith: My Journey in the Quest for Justice in Repressive Kenya, 1958-2015,* Nairobi: Vita Books

Patel, Z (2006). *Unquiet: The Life and Times of Makhan Singh.* Nairobi: Zand Graphics.

Rattansi, Pyarally 2006. 'Remembering Makhan Singh, One of the Great Heroes of Kenya'. First Makhan Singh Memorial Lecture. Taifa Hall, University of Nairobi, Nairobi, Kenya, 20 March.

Rocker, [1938] 1989, Anarcho-syndicalism, pp. 110-114.

Rosemont, F. 2003. Joe Hill: *The IWW and the Making of a Revolutionary Working-Class Counterculture.* Chicago: Charles H. Kerr.

Stichter, 1975, 'Workers, Trade Unions, and the Mau Mau Rebellion', pp. 265-266.

Van der Walt, L (2013). 'Makhan Singh, Ghadar, the IWW and

Communism: Legacy and Relevance to African Trade Unions Today.' In Patel, Z. and Van der Wlat, L (eds) *Building African Working Class Unity: Makhan Singh Memorial Lectures*
Zeleza, T (1993). 'The Strike Movement in Colonial Kenya: The Era of the General Strikes.' *Transafrican Journal of History, Vol. 22* (1993), pp. 1-23;

Makhan Singh – A Retrospection

Pheroze Nowrojee[38]

In the space of five months between January and May 1950, Makhan Singh changed the direction of politics in Kenya. He turned it from seeking greater representation and participation within colonial rule, to the goal of ending colonial rule and thereby bringing in independence and freedom. This he did by making two statements. They were political calls for action. They were also prophecies for that decade of the 1950s. The two statements were issued within those few months in the following circumstances.

In 1950, the Colonial Government announced that Nairobi, till then a Municipality, would become a city. This was to be done by the grant of a Royal Charter, which would be presented in Nairobi by the Duke of Gloucester, the King's brother. There would be great and extensive celebrations. The political purpose was to underscore the firm British hold over the colony, and also over their declining but still vital sphere of influence in the western Indian Ocean. Internally, it was to reassure the settlers of the promise of British Rule in the long-term foreseeable future.

On March 20, 1950, Fred Kubai, as President of the East African Trade Union Congress, and Makhan Singh, as its Secretary-General, issued a joint statement of the Congress, calling on all workers to boycott the celebrations. They said, "There are two Nairobis – the Nairobi of the rich and that of the poor."[39] They continued, "The status of the latter Nairobi has not changed and there was therefore nothing for them to celebrate."[40]

Three weeks later, on Sunday, April 13, 1950, a critical Joint Meeting of the Kenya African Union (KAU) (then chaired by Jomo Kenyatta), and the East African Indian National Congress (EAINC), was held at Kaloleni Social Hall, Nairobi. A joint resolution was presented to

38 Senior Counsel, Co-Chair of the Asian African Heritage Trust, Nairobi, author of *Pio Gama Pinto, Patriot for Social Justice* (Nairobi, Sasa Sema, 2007).

39 Zarina Patel (2006): *Unquiet: The Life and Times of Makhan Singh* (Nairobi, Kenya Human Rights Commission, 2006), 217.

40 Ibid, 218.

condemn the racist settler agitation against African constitutional advance in neighbouring Tanganyika. Speaking in support of the resolution to the audience of over 17,000 persons, Makhan Singh said:

> "... the real solution of the problem [of colonial rule] is not this or that small reform, but the complete Independence and sovereignty of the East African territories and the establishment in all of these territories of democratic governments elected by the people, and responsible to the people of these territories only, and that the solution should be implemented at an early date.[41]

In a further article of May 1, 1950 in celebration of Labour Day, Makhan Singh renewed the call for the boycott.

Makhan Singh was thus a threat not only to colonial rule in Kenya, but to British interests on the international stage. Because of the latter, the British saw control of Kenya also as a matter of British security (as distinct from the security of Kenya itself.)

British interests in the region lay in their financial and naval base in Aden, and in the British Indian Ocean Territories, both immediately affecting their naval control of the ocean and hold over trade and military routes to Singapore, Malaya and Hong Kong.

On the African continent itself, the old ambitions to salvage and consolidate the wounded Empire by a formal making of a new dominion remained unabated at the end of the Second World War in 1945. "The opposition to Haile Selassie, to his role in the liberation of Ethiopia and to his return to Addis Ababa, came from the military-colonial group led by Sir Philip Mitchell, Chief Political Officer for the Administration of Occupied Enemy Territory [Ethiopia], under General Earl Wavell, Commander-in-Chief, Middle East. ... Reflecting the attitudes of the British Colonial Service these officials would have re-drawn the map of East Africa so as to join the Sudan to Kenya through a British Horn [of Africa] consisting of Eritrea, Ethiopia and the French, British and Italian Somaliland"[42] and

41 Ibid, 222.

42 John H Spencer, *Ethiopia At Bay* (Algonac MI, Reference Publications, 1984), p.94. John H Spencer, an American, was on Haile Sellasie's staff since the Italian invasion of Ethiopia in 1936 and was with Haile Sellasie in the Sudan and Ethiopia between 1941 and 1945, and then when the Emperor resumed his reign from Addis Ababa. He was well placed to assess the conduct and

thereby to extend British control south from the Red Sea through Kenya to South Africa.

At this very time, Makhan Singh was politically active and was under British detention in India. Two years later, when Makhan Singh returned in 1947 from India to fresh political activity in Kenya, Sir Philip Mitchell had already been appointed Governor of Kenya, having earlier also been the Governor of Uganda. Makhan Singh, in communist activity since 1934 against British imperialism and oppression in India and Kenya, understood well the strategic choreography of these British moves, and their totally negative impact on any advance to independence for Kenya.

It became Makhan Singh's political agenda to ensure the prevention of the British expansion of dominion as aforementioned and to immediately entrench the demand of independence as the aim of the African political movements in East Africa, particularly Kenya, together with the organisation of this through the trade unions and the principal existing political parties, Kenya African Union (KAU) and the East African Indian National Congress (EAINC)... This explains his two statements and their early timing. In turn, Sir Philip Mitchell and the British understood well Makhan Singh's movements. The speed with which they removed him to put him into detention in 1950 confirms this.

Further, the division of labour in the Cold War in the 1950s left the defence against the spread of communism in these areas to the British. Thus, issues relating to communism and communists in these areas was a British responsibility (which they quickly shared with the South African Boer regime). This was also reflected in the fact that Makhan Singh's own case was dealt with and came to the Governor-in-Council in 1961, for his release from detention, not from the Kenya Police or Home Affairs but from the Kenya Ministry of Defence.[43]

His two statements encompassed all these issues and established a threat to the British in both Kenya and internationally. The British thus

---

imperial purposes of Sir Philip Mitchell and the British military-colonial group who entered Ethiopia in 1941 and kept Haile Sellasie out of Addis Ababa for years with these purposes in mind.

43 Singh, Makhan: T*he Autobiography of Makhan Singh and Documents Relating to His Release*. (Nairobi, Asian African Heritage Trust, 2015) 16th October 1961, p.42.

considered both these statements so powerful, so widely disseminated and so well-received by the workers, as indeed they were, that only 14 days after the last of them, Makhan Singh was placed in detention at Lokitaung, Northern Frontier Province, arriving there on May 15, 1950. And the reaction to his arrest and detention confirmed the British assessments of their substantial effect. His arrest was met by a national general strike by workers which lasted for more than a week. The British themselves wrote:

> Although no serious incidents or injuries occurred, the strike, which was also remarkable for its intimidation, showed that Makhan Singh's influence and organizational ability were considerable.[44]

And this was while he was already in custody! It is therefore not surprising that he was not released for the following 11½ years till October 18, 1961. He was the longest serving detainee in the independence struggle.

Makhan Singh's political work was with a clear theoretical base and long experience in Kenya and India, backed by communist analysis of, and planning against, British oppression. This was a formidable combination, with unyielding action towards targets of social justice. Though historians since 1963 have not fully appreciated this pre-eminence of his, his British opposites paid him the compliment of never underestimating him, or of not taking into account what a free Makhan Singh could do in a free Kenya against British interests, even after 11 years of detention. Indeed, at the time of the consideration in 1961 of his intended release, the British did take these factors into account, yet finally released him.[45]

*

Makhan Singh is also an inspiration to all Kenyans in respect of the constancy of his beliefs. "During his detention all sorts of pressures (not physical) were brought upon him to make him either leave Kenya or change his attitude. Makhan Singh did neither. On the day of his release, he openly declared that he was still a communist and would continue his political and trade union activities."[46]

---

44 Ibid, p.39.

45 Secret Document, Memorandum by the Minister of Defence,10th October 1961. (Archival Documents, 1961) in The Autobiography of Makhan Singh and Documents Relating to His Release Makhan Singh (Nairobi, Asian African Heritage Trust, 2015), p.41-42.

46 Ibid, p.28.

How was he held in the estimation of the African political leadership? At the time of his immigration trials in Nyeri, in early 1950, Makhan Singh's advocate, Chanan Singh, recalls that when he and Makhan Singh came to Nyeri on the first day of the trial, they were surprised to find waiting outside the court Senior Chief Koinange wa Mbiyu and many of his followers. Senior Chief Koinange explained to Chanan Singh that he had come to Nyeri to appear as a witness for Makhan Singh as to his desirability as a permanent resident of Kenya, (there was no 'citizenship of Kenya' at that time). This was the highest endorsement by the highest freedom authority, the Senior Chief. In the end, no witnesses to that effect were however taken.

Makhan Singh is a model for another duty on political work in the freedom struggle: the recording of the struggle, and the propagation of the demands and ideals of the freedom movement. After his release, Makhan Singh himself wrote two books on the history of trade unions in Kenya and their struggle: *History of Kenya's Trade Union Movement to 1952* (Nairobi, East African Publishing House,1969) and *Kenya's Trade Unions 1952 to 1956* (Nairobi, Uzima Publishers, 1980). In addition, each year, Makhan Singh wrote a paper for the annual conference of the Historical Association of Kenya and was also the author of the chapter, 'The East African Trade Union Congress 1949-1950' in Bethwell A Ogot (ed.) *Politics and Nationalism in Colonial Kenya* (Nairobi, East African Publishing House, 1972, at 207).

Makhan Singh's work not only remains pertinent but needs to be studied more closely. The major statements that he made in 1950 (that we have examined earlier), set out his political persona. In respect of national issues, they were underlining the danger of unchecked inequality within Kenya; and on the international front, they pointed out the dangers of continuing imperial control, foreseeing the neo-colonialism that would come later.

They also manifest his clear theoretical base and his clear political programmes. They remained consistent throughout his life – in Kenya, in India, then again in Kenya. His unyielding commitments to the freedom of Kenya and the freedom of India bore fruit within his lifetime.[47] Throughout, he kept a focus on the proletariat as the principal and proper agent of change. Hence, to fulfil his political aims, his active political work was constantly directed on the establishment of the trade union movement and trade unions.

He never joined the Communist Party of India (CPI), (there was none in East Africa at the time, but there is now, a registered party, since the Second Liberation). But he did join the Kenya and East African political parties, and even held office within them. More importantly, he worked to have the EAINC and KAU take joint political steps and programmes, which unity the British recognised in their colonies as the most dangerous development to their continued control of Africa. Makhan Singh saw it early. He saw also the use of coordinated policies and action not only between political parties but also between trade unions and political parties.

Makhan Singh, like all the Independence heroes and resistance groups, has suffered erasure. Bildad Kaggia, Pio Gama Pinto, Senior Chief Koinange, Oginga Odinga, and the thousands of former freedom fighters released from the camps. All have been erased from Kenyan history. This was done by both Kenyatta and by the British, the former to impress that he was the only bringer of Uhuru. And by the latter, to impress that nothing untoward had ever happened anyway. And thereby, in turn, they erased the settlers from Kenyan and colonial history.

Our task is not to keep bemoaning this, but to reverse the erasure. It is a hard process. It requires continuous work, planned research and studies, and re-dissemination of basic facts. To Kenyatta and the British, erasure however was an easy process: The Kenya Government had a monopoly of the radio; they had a monopoly of television; there were no other stations in either media. These two

---

47 *The Autobiography of Makhan Singh and Documents Relating to His Release* (Nairobi, Asian African Heritage Trust, 2015). In this autobiography, at p.24, he writes (in the third person, in which the whole of the fragmentary autobiography is written), "He left India for Kenya in the first week of August and celebrated India's Independence Day on the 15th of August, 1947, [mid-ocean] while still on the SS Shirola. One main aim of Makhan Singh's life, the freedom of India, had been achieved." And on p.30, he writes, "He is now nearing the attainment, on 12th December 1963, of the second main goal of his life – the complete independence of East Africa".

were the only widespread means of countrywide recognition. Further, these means only gave coverage to President Kenyatta daily and to his office holders as directed. None of the victims of erasure were in any case given any public office, and so they were never covered anyway. (Save when assassinated). But there was deeper damage by Kenyatta: omission of these figures in the school and university syllabi; omission from national day speeches and omission from street names.

One of the ways to begin the process of restoring his proper place in Kenya's history is through the trade unions. Trade unions have to establish scholarships in the name of Fred Kubai and Makhan Singh, the founders of the movement. And certainly, by the recovery of their speeches and writings from the 1950s. These are small steps, but they need big patriots to start this work.

Reflections on the Revolutionary Legacy of Makhan Singh

Shiraz Durrani[48]

Makhan Singh played a crucial role in Kenyan people's struggle against colonialism and imperialism. His was not a narrow perspective of gaining a limited political independence under imperialism. He saw the economic as well as political liberation of working people and the achievement of a society based on principles of social justice and equality as the ultimate goals of trade union and the nationalist struggles. He saw the achievement of economic and political rights of working people, marginalised by colonialism, imperialism and capitalism, as the primary goal of the liberation struggle. His base for achieving his goals was the trade union movement, which he did much to organise and

---

48 Shiraz Durrani is a Kenyan political exile living in London. He has worked at the University of Nairobi as well as at a number of public libraries in Britain. He then lectured at the London Metropolitan University. Shiraz has written many books and articles on aspects of Kenyan history and on politics of information in the context of colonialism, capitalism and imperialism. Some of his articles are available at https://independent.academia.edu/DurraniShiraz and books at: https://www.africanbookscollective.com/search-results?form.keywords=shiraz+durrani

radicalise along class lines. He realised that the economic demands of working people could be met only by winning the political as well as the economic struggles. He was among those Kenyans who saw clearly what the needs of the time were. He devoted his life totally to developing a vision of a society that was fair and just for working people. He helped set up appropriate organisational frameworks – in trade unions and in the political field – as a way of ensuring the achievement of his vision. He developed appropriate forms of communication to raise class consciousness among people. This ensured that people understood the working of capitalism and took necessary action at different stages of their struggle. He lived by the principles he believed in, making sacrifices which very few people were – or are — ready to make.

Makhan Singh: The Early Years

Makhan Singh's background in Kenya and India prepared him well for the important role he was to play in both countries. His autobiography (Singh, 1963) provides some details on his early Kenya experience:

> In June 1931, Makhan Singh began working in his father's printing press ... In March 1935 he was elected Secretary of the Indian Trade Union. In the following month he, along with others, induced the Indian Trade Union to change its name to Labour Trade Union of Kenya and to open its doors to all workers irrespective of race, religion, colour or creed ... he remained General Secretary until August 1949 when he was elected President (p.142).

His autobiography further relates his works in India:

> Towards the end of December 1939, he [Makhan Singh] left for India, there to study working class conditions and the functioning of trade unionism in Bombay and Ahmedabad ... in the first week of March (1940), he addressed a large mass meeting of about 30,000 Bombay workers and strikers. A few days later he attended the Ramgarh Session of the Indian National Congress as an African delegate (p.144).

Makhan Singh was totally immersed in the freedom struggle and in the working class movement in India. For this, he was arrested by the British colonial authorities on May 5, 1940. No charges were brought against him, as his autobiography notes. It was during his detention that he strengthened his links with communist, socialist and other revolutionary leaders from all over India. He was one of the 140 detainees who went on hunger strike in 1941. He was released from detention in July 1942, but was kept under restriction within the village of Gharjakh until January 1945. In all, he was under detention and restriction in India for more than four-and-a-half years.

He then worked as a sub-editor of *Jang-i-Azadi* [Struggle for Freedom], the weekly organ of the Punjab Committee of the Communist Party of India, until he left for Kenya in August 1947. As his autobiography notes, "one main aim of Makhan Singh's life, the freedom of India, had been achieved" (p. 145). He next turned to his other aim – freedom and liberation in Kenya. His exposure to communism, to experiences in organisational work and mass action in India had prepared him well for the struggle in Kenya, both at the level of trade unionism and in the political struggle for independence. The experiences with which Makhan Singh came to Kenya enriched and developed the anti-colonial, anti-capitalism, anti-imperialist struggles in the country.

Power Behind the Scenes

Makhan Singh took a principled stand in the struggle for the liberation of Kenya. It was this that made the colonial administration determined to take him and his ideas out of circulation by detaining and restricting him for the longest period that anyone in Kenya had suffered at the hands of colonialism. The aim was to isolate him from his base support – the working class, the trade union and the national liberation movement. Makhan Singh was a victim of the same colonial and imperialist system that today condemns hundreds of people to illegal detention in the US-run or inspired prisons all over the world. The reasons for Makhan Singh's long restriction are revealed in secret Minutes of the 77th Meeting of the Council of Ministers held on October 18, 1961:

> The Governor pointed out that Makhan Singh had not at any time been tried for any offence, although he had now been in restriction for a period of 11 years. On the other hand, there was no doubt that he was a potentially dangerous person and there was evidence that he would never change his political views (Kenya, Colony and Protectorate, 1961).

In the twisted logic of the colonial world, standing up for one's political principles was considered "dangerous" and deserving long detention – no matter that the person may have committed no offences. The foregoing document then goes on to explain why colonialism thought that Makhan Singh was so dangerous to its rule:

> There was at present a spate of subversive societies throughout the colony and, in addition, there was within the groups which formed the Opposition in Legislative Council tense political situation brought about by the struggle between the constitutionalists and the revolutionaries. The immediate release of such person as Makhan Singh would tend to strengthen the revolutionaries... Makhan Singh had in particular a history of influence in the trade union movement and if released there was a possibility of his becoming a power behind the scenes to turn the movement in a revolutionary direction.

Thus emerges the reason for Makhan Singh's persecution. He represented the revolutionary strand of the Kenyan liberation movement whereas the colonial administration tolerated or supported the 'constitutionalists', who were considered the best way for colonialism to morph into neo-colonialism and to support imperialism. From the colonial perspective, its repressive actions had helped to create a neo-colonial state in Kenya and were thus successful. The stand that Makhan Singh took would have led to real liberation for working people of Kenya, and that was considered unacceptable to the imperialist powers. That the 'independent' governments of Kenya after 1963 continued the colonial-period treatment of Makhan Singh as a dangerous revolutionary is a testament to the success of the imperialist vision of the new Kenya. It is indeed ironic that Makhan Singh, who was the first to demand and struggle for 'uhuru sasa' became a victim of the uhuru government itself.

Makhan Singh is not alone in this imperialist-imposed isolation and marginalisation. One hears little of many other prominent activists who achieved much and sacrificed their lives in many cases for the cause of national liberation. Among them are revolutionaries like Dedan Kimaathi, Chege Kibachia, Bildad Kaggia, Fred Kubai, and Pio Gama Pinto among thousands others who took up arms and resisted colonialism. In addition, there were revolutionaries throughout the period of British colonialism in Kenya who stood against the might of the colonial empire. Their histories, as that of Makhan Singh and Mau Mau, remain hidden to this day.

Early Influences on Makhan Singh

Makhan Singh's autobiography (1963) mentions early influences on Makhan Singh which came to prominence in later years:

> During the period of his schooling in Nairobi, Makhan Singh continued taking interest in world events and was influenced by the workers' and peasants' movements (both communist and socialist) and trade union struggles. At the same time, he also commenced composing and reciting poems in Punjabi on religious, social and political subjects with emphasis on the struggle for freedom (pp.141--142).

Added to this early learning, Makhan Singh continued 'a serious study of political literature of all types' (Singh, 1963) when he started work at his father's printing press in 1931. He continued his learning and links with various communist organisations in South Africa, Britain and India and studied their documents. Kenya had an early taste of anti-imperialist movements in the Ghadar movement[49] and Makhan Singh developed his own thinking and links with such organisations. Indeed many Ghadar activists were hanged by British colonial authorities, while many others were trained in Moscow in revolutionary theory and practice.

So strong was his own influence on events in Kenya that Makhan Singh was targeted by imperialism as the source of major concern for them, as Kinyatti (2008) notes:

> Makhan Singh was imprisoned without trial and restricted at Lokitaung until 1961. He had committed a double crime: he was a communist and a leader of the trade union movement. Since he was the key leader of the anti-imperialist labour movement, his banishment to Lokitaung, the imperialist occupiers thought, would weaken its leadership (p.99).

A fuller, systemically conducted research into the early influences on Makhan Singh is beyond the scope of this article, yet it is urgently needed. That task is made easier by the vast resource now available in the Makhan Singh Archives, Patel (2006) and other resources on the history of Kenya – not least the recently released Colonial Files.

---

49 Further details on the Ghadar movement are available in Chandan (2015), Durrani (2006) and Patel (2006).

But what is clear is that Makhan Singh's study, learning, experiences and activities enabled him to see and act on the working-class perspectives in the on-going contradiction against colonialism, capitalism and imperialism. In this, he was a great educational influence on generations of activists.

Class, Trade Union and Worker Rights

Makhan Singh saw class divisions and class struggles as the primary aspects of resistance to colonialism and to ensuring that the interests of workers, peasants and people of Kenya were at the forefront of an independent country. This was a turning point in the struggle for liberation in Kenya. Colonialism had succeeded in previous periods to divide people's struggles along 'tribal' or racial or regional levels, thereby dividing forces of resistance. Makhan Singh was able to see through such divisive tactics. He saw the struggle as a class struggle and emphasised the need to politicise the working class, unite them with other progressive classes and wage a struggle that would remove the causes of poverty and injustice from the country.

He used his experience in press work and his communication skills to present to workers and working people of Kenya an alternative perspective from that projected by colonialism and imperialism. His study of the history of working class struggles in the world had shown that capitalism was not the only way to organise a society and that socialism was the way to establish justice and equality. The experience from USSR was a clear example of how an alternative system could work. For this to have an impact in Kenya, it was necessary to establish various methods of communication, including newspapers, leaflets and oral channels as well as creative means such as poetry, among others, in the languages used by the people. But the crucial aspect was the content of such messages. The leaflets reproduced hereunder, issued by EATUC, for example, were clear on the class nature of the struggle in Kenya:

The Struggle between Capitalists and Workers has Started in Earnest

STRUGGLE BETWEEN CAPITALISTS AND WORKERS HAS STARTED IN EARNEST

Our worker comrades! Come forward! March ahead! If you do not march ahead today, then remember that you will be crushed under the heels of capitalists tomorrow. Workers should have a united stand and should stand up strongly against the capitalists so that they should not ever have the courage to attempt to exploit workers again, nor to take away workers' rights from them.

Note: The workers of M/s Karsan Ladha have gone on strike for higher wages. It has been reported that the strike situation is becoming serious. This has now become a question of life or death for workers.

- LABOUR TRADE UNION OF KENYA, November 29, 1936[88]

Makhan Singh Archives, University of Nairobi, Nairobi (translated from Gujarati by the author).

LTUEA HANDBILL, 1935 (KHALSA PRESS)

WORKERS' MASS MEETING

Workers' mass meeting

A workers' mass meeting will be held on Saturday, 16th January, at 5.00 p.m. in the Ramgharia Plot (Campos Ribero St.) to decide effective methods to achieve the demands of Railway artisans and the demand of 25% increase in wages from 1st April. Please do attend. Long Live Workers' Unity - Makhan Singh, Sec. Labour Trade Unions

Terms such as capitalists, workers, comrades, exploit, struggle, workers' rights indicate a departure from the way that Kenyan people had struggled against colonialism and imperialism in the past. Makhan Singh brought about a paradigm shift in people's thinking about their situation – and in the ways of combating this powerful enemy. So powerful was this message that imperialism had no arguments to counter its thinking. All they could do was wage a massive war against the people of Kenya and to remove the person who started this revolution in people's thinking – Makhan Singh – for over 11 years from the midst of people he led to this new way of thinking.

Achieving Workers' Rights

The first level at which Makhan Singh fought was to achieve workers' rights. It should be noted that resistance to Portuguese and British colonialism has been a feature of the entire colonial period in Kenya. Recording workers' resistance was as much a part of the struggle as organising strikes. Without such records, working class history is forgotten and lost. Singh (1969), therefore, recorded some of the earliest strikes thus:

- 1900: railway workers strike – interestingly this was initiated by European subordinate staff and later on "probably joined by some Indian and African workers." The strike started in Mombasa and spread to other centres along the railway line.
- 1902: strike by African police constables.
- 1908: strikes of African workers at a Government farm at Mazeras and those engaged in loading railway engines.
- 1908: strike of railway Indian workers at Kilindini harbor.
- 1908: strike by rickshaw-pullers in Nairobi.
- 1912: strike by African boat workers in Mombasa.
- 1912: strike by employees of the railway goods shed in Nairobi.
- 1912: persistent refusal by thousands of African workers on settlers' farms (pp. 6-7).

Thus there has been a long history of worker activism in Kenya together with the formation of unions, for example, the Indian Trades Union in Mombasa and "probably in Nairobi" in 1914, the Railway Artisan Union (1922), the Trade Union Committee of Mombasa (1930), and the Workers Protective Society of Kenya (1931), the Indian Trade Union (1933) which changed its name to Kenya Indian Labour Trade Union. But unions faced a number of problems that made their survival difficult. Two important impediments were mentioned by Makhan Singh (1969), indicating his own role in consolidating radical trade unions in Kenya:

> The basic difficulty was the usual one. There was no team of workers who, after having been elected officials of the union, were prepared to devote their time regularly and fearlessly to making the union function in a spirit of co-operation, unity, sacrifice and service. The reasons for the lack of such a team were not hard to find. The trade union functionaries from the very beginning had to face the general hostility of employers and the colonial rulers. The threat of victimisation by employers and/or deportation by the government was always there (p.47).

Makhan Singh (1969) goes on to the second impediment:

> There was no trade union legislation. The nature of the existing labour legislation was such that there could only be discouragement for the formation of trade unions. The migratory character of workers made the continuity of a union nearly impossible. Industry was undeveloped. There was none worth the name except the railway. That made the employment of a worker generally short-lived, so that he was compelled to go from job to job, workshop to workshop, town to town. All these factors equally affected the trade unionists. So it was no wonder that the Kenya Indian Labour Trade union was in the same quandary as some of its predecessors (p.47).

But this time, there was a new element in the oppressive situation: there was someone prepared to 'to devote their time regularly and fearlessly to making the union function in a 'spirit of co-operation, unity, sacrifice and service'. Enter Makhan Singh, who became the biggest threat to employers and the colonial government. They detained him for over 11 years because they saw a great threat in him. Just one individual, with his clear vision, commitment and willingness to devote his life to the struggle and to make personal and family sacrifices was sufficient to threaten the foundation of the entire colonial-imperialist endeavour. Colonialism-imperialism found it easy to aim their bullets at armed and unarmed Mau Mau combatants and activists; they found it impossible to shoot down the ideas, the vision and the undaunted stand of Makhan Singh.

Makhan Singh's unique qualities did not go unnoticed among TU activists of the time. Again Makhan Singh (1969) takes up the narrative:

> About two months after the formation of the Kenya Indian Labour Trade Union, it became obvious that it would be difficult for the union to continue to function. In February 1935, Makhan Singh was asked by the railway artisans if he could give a hand to help the union. He agreed (p.49).

Makhan Singh made his presence felt in a matter of weeks. Within five weeks, the union was made non-racial. Its name was changed to the Labour Trade Union of Kenya (LTUK). 'Its membership was made open to all workers irrespective of race, religion, caste, creed, colour or tribe... New officials were appointed with Gulam Mohamed (railway) as President and Makhan Singh as Honorary Secretary' (Singh, 1969, p.49).

Thus was addressed the first obstacle mentioned earlier. Colonialism had kept the working-class divided on the basis of the colour of their skin or locality, not allowing nationwide organisations. Now, Labour Trade Union of Kenya enters the scene as a nationwide organisation, open to all workers. The result was a much stronger organisation that was difficult to 'divide and rule' as per colonial and employer practice. Makhan Singh (1969) recalls:

> The LTUK began to function in earnest. An office was rented... it was furnished with necessary office equipment, including a typewriter and a rotary cyclostyle machine. Meetings of the management committee and the constitution sub-committee began to take place regularly and the enrolment of members commenced (p.50).

Thus a functioning organisation was created by Makhan Singh and it was this that changed the working-class scene in Kenya. The acquisition of printing facilities enabled the trade union movement to keep workers informed about its struggles and strikes. Thus leaflets in various languages were widely circulated in Nairobi as well as throughout the areas covered by the railway line, being distributed by worker activists employed on the railways. Thus, another disadvantage faced by workers – lack of communication facilities and system – which had hampered earlier actions was removed by the LTUK.

Among the early actions of LTUK was to address a major worker grievance: long worker hours. Some highlights are provided by Makhan Singh (1969):

> The LTUK took up the problem of long working hours that was very prevalent at that time... on 10th August 1935 a resolution was passed by a mass meeting of workers [which] 'condemns the action of those employers... who are weakening the workers physically and are increasing unemployment... hence it strongly demands from all the employers that in no case should keep their employees at work for more than eight hours a day, and wages should remain as they are (p.53).

The increasingly militant union then set a date in October 1936 for its demands on the working hours to be accepted by employers. It is a reflection of the success of the union's strategy and hard work that their demands were met. The union gained the support of African workers as well and large numbers began to join the union. 'The effect of the success was felt all over Kenya and in Uganda and Tanzania, too. The membership of the union went up more than 1,000', observed Makhan Singh (1969).

Following the success of this campaign, the union 'decided in a mass meeting of Nairobi workers that notices be given to employers that the wages of all employees be increased by 25 per cent from April 1, 1937" (Singh, 1969). A strike was declared to achieve this aim:
In accordance with the plan, the strike began on Thursday, the April, 1 1937. It was a complete strike. A strike committee was formed. Picketing was organised. A free kitchen was started, where strikers and unemployed could have their food (p.60).

The strike to support these demands lasted 62 days and ended in success: 'The employers agreed in writing to a wage-increase ranging from 15 to 22 per cent, an eight-hour day and reinstatement of all the strikers' (p.63).

While this was a great achievement, there was another significant outcome of the strike. Singh (1963) recalls the impact of the 1937 strike for wage increase:

> The result of the victory was that Union's membership rose to about 2,500... another result was that the government came to the conclusion that the Trade Union Movement in Kenya had come to stray and that trade union legislation was necessary. A Trade Union Bill was published in the middle of May 1937 when the strike was still continuing and it became an Ordinance in August. The Union was registered under it in September 1937 (pp.142-143).

Thus an important requirement for any struggle, the formation of an organisation, was met.

In this way, the two obstacles mentioned earlier facing the trade union movement were removed. Kenya had reached a new stage in its anti-colonialism, anti-imperialism struggles.

It is of interest to note that while Makhan Singh played a crucial role in this transformation, he worked without payment. Nor does he even mention his role in the history of the period. His biography (Singh, 1963) and his two books (Singh, M 1969 and 1980) do not mention him in all the activities he initiated and guided, giving credit to union actions.

Linking Economic and Political Struggle

An important contribution that Makhan Singh made to the struggle for liberation in Kenya was to link the two aspects of a liberation struggle that imperialism sought to keep separate. These were economic and political aspects. Makhan Singh believed that in order to meet the economic demands of working people, it was essential to win political power first. It was only thus that foundations for an entirely different society could be laid. This is how Makhan Singh saw the connections between economic demands of workers and the struggle for national liberation:

> Kenya's trade union movement has always been a part of her national struggle for resisting British imperialist colonial rule, for winning national independence, for consolidating the independence after winning it, and for bringing prosperity to the workers and people of Kenya (Singh, 1969, Introduction).

Makhan Singh was the first person to make a call for independence in Kenya in 1950, but he was clear that winning independence was not an end in itself; independence had to be consolidated to ensure prosperity for workers and people of Kenya. Ouma and Mutua (2006) explain the two aspects of Makhan Singh's work:

> The legacy of Makhan Singh points to the centrality of trade unions as one of the major epicentres of democracy. Singh wanted workers to get organised on both practical and strategic issues. The practical issues varied from housing, wages, working conditions, health, and safety among others. Strategically, he was conscious of the fact that colonialism and crude capitalism were the key foundations for the privation of workers. That is why in 1950, Singh proposed a resolution urging complete independence and sovereignty of the East African territories as the only viable solution to suffering of the people (pp. ix-x).

Thus Makhan Singh brought together the two strands in the Kenya liberation movement – trade union and politics – which capitalism seeks to keep separate, even to this day. "He first came to prominence as secretary of the Labour Trade Union of Kenya when he organised a two-month strike in Nairobi," writes Sicherman (1990, p. 178) referring to the first aspect of his work, the other being his 1950 call for independence.

Makhan Singh "embarrassed Kenyatta and Mathu by calling for immediate independence in Kenya at a joint meeting of the Kenya African Union and the East African Indian National Congress in April 1950" (Thorp, quoted in Sicherman, 1990). Seidenberg (1983, p.104) records that Makhan Singh stated that "the British Government had declared the independence of India, Burma and Ceylon; similarly it should immediately declare the independence of the East African territories." Seidenberg (1983) further quotes Ambu Patel: "This was the first time in the history of the freedom struggle in Kenya that anyone had actually dared to make such a demand in public."

Seidenberg (1983) sums up Makhan Singh's contribution to the trade union movement in Kenya, as well as to the struggle for independence:

> With the return of Makhan Singh in August 1947, the trade union movement also acquired a radical wing. Having spent eight years in India actively participating in the trade union movement and the political struggle for independence, Makhan Singh was well-

equipped to breathe new life into Kenya's labour and freedom campaign. The Labour Trade Union of East Africa formed in 1937 and later the larger East African Trade Union Congress (EATUC) formed in May 1949 became the nerve centres for activities of the more militant Asians. From 1947 until 1952, when all trade union activities were proscribed, Makhan Singh worked in behind-the-scenes activities with prominent African trade unionists including Bildad Kaggia, Aggrey Minya and Tom Mboya (p.97).

The colonial administration used the period before independence in 1963 to embed a system of laws that ensured that the economic struggles of working people were kept separate from their political struggles. Kubai (1969) sees the significance of the linking of these two aspects:

> I have always encountered critics who believe that our trade unions in those days were not trade unions at all in the real sense because they were politically formed and were not confined to industrial collective bargaining. This book[50] informs them the reasons why it was necessary for the trade unions of those days to conduct their struggles not only industrially but also politically and to take an active part in the national struggle for Kenya's independence (Kubai, 1969).

It is important to see how Makhan Singh and the trade union movement linked the economic and political struggles. The political basis of his trade union work was created by the very conditions under which capitalism operates. Ouma and Mutua (2006) see the connection:

> Singh's political work in the trade union movement was a response to the repressive colonial state generally and the labour law regime in particular. Under the colonial state – and its post-colonial successor – Kenya was imprisoned in labour laws that were designed to cheapen and exploit so-called native labour. This was the trend worldwide in the relationship between labour and capital. No wonder workers have been at the forefront of the human rights struggle over the centuries ... Makhan Singh created the building blocks and pillars of the trade union movement in Kenya (p. viii).

50 Referring to Makhan Singh (1969): History of Kenya's Trade Union Movement to 1952. Nairobi: EAPH.

Such was the political and economic background that created the objective reality that Makhan Singh and the trade union movement faced. But external factors themselves do not create change. Internal conditions have to be ready to take advantage of the conditions if there is going to be a major social change. Makhan Singh and others working with him helped to create appropriate organisations and trained activists to take the struggle to the next stage by putting their ideas into practice.

Makhan Singh and the progressive trade union movement he helped consolidate and radicalise recognised that for power to be attained and used effectively in the interest of working classes, some essential elements were necessary: an appropriate ideology and vision of the desired society, an organisation that could lead people to achieve its vision, effective leadership supported by well informed and experienced activists. Without these essentials, movements and revolutions can – and are – diverted by enemies of working people, as Milne (2013) points out in the context of today's struggles:

> In the era of neoliberalism, when the ruling elite has hollowed out democracy and ensured that whoever you vote for you get the same, politically inchoate protest movements are bound to flourish. They have crucial strengths: they can change moods, ditch policies and topple governments. But without socially rooted organisation and clear political agendas, they can flare and fizzle, or be vulnerable to hijacking or diversion by more entrenched and powerful forces.

And that is exactly what happened to the revolutionary trade union and liberation movement in Kenya. While the progressive forces are yet to learn the full lesson of this process of marginalising popular movements by elites and imperialism, colonialism was well prepared to divert Kenyan resistance and render it ineffective by colluding with the elite it had nurtured during the entire colonial period. It was this elite that was handed state power at independence. Kenya still has to wage – and win — the second phase of its struggle for total liberation. Lessons from earlier failures and experiences from other countries need to be urgently studied and applied today. This is also taking place in different forms in South Africa, which has many parallels with the situation in Kenya in terms of this process that imperialism resorts to of rendering radical movements and organisations ineffective. It is important to hear the progressive voice from South African trade unions and activists so as to apply appropriate lessons to the situation in Kenya today, but also to understand its history correctly. What Kasrils (2013) says about South Africa can also be applied to Kenya:

> South Africa's liberation struggle reached a high point but not its zenith when we overcame apartheid rule. Back then, our hopes were high for our country given its modern industrial economy, strategic mineral resources (not only gold and diamonds), and a working class and organised trade union movement with a rich tradition of struggle. But that optimism overlooked the tenacity of the international capitalist system. From 1991 to 1996, the battle for the ANC's soul got under way, and was eventually lost to corporate power: we were entrapped by the neoliberal economy – or, as some today cry out, we "sold our people down the river".

It was the same process of entrapment by neoliberal forces that enabled the international capitalist system to subjugate Kenya. As a result, radical leaders such as Kimaathi, Makhan Singh, Bildad Kaggia, Fred Kubai, Pio Gama Pinto, progressive organisations such as Mau Mau and the radical trade unions, and vision of a just and equal society that they aspired to were forcibly removed from the scene by a triumphant imperialism.

*

An example of how Makhan Singh linked economic and political demands of workers reveals his approach. It relates to the political demand for independence for East Africa. Seidenberg (1983) recalls the joint Indian National Congress and KAU (Kenya African Union) meeting in 1950 in response to the European Electors' Union's so-called Kenya Plan for the establishment of a British East African Dominion:

> Then Makhan Singh took the floor ... he boldly moved an addendum to the resolution declaring that "complete independence and sovereignty of the East African territories" was the "real solution" and the one which should be implemented "at an early" date". In an impassioned speech, he said that the time had come for the people to unite and to demand in a single voice that the country was theirs and that no foreign power had the right to rule over it. That should be the aim of Africans,

Indians and progressive Europeans. The British Government had declared the independence of India, Burma and Ceylon; similarly, it should immediately declare the independence of the East African territories. This was the first time in the history of the freedom struggle in Kenya that anyone had actually dared to make such a demand in public (p.104).

It is clear from this example that for Makhan Singh, the economic demands of working people could only be fully met once they had political power to make appropriate policies independent of corporate and finance capital interests. The real issue is which class has power to make policies, rules and regulations and in the interest of which class is the state power used. Workers' demands could only start to be met once there was political independence, hence Makhan Singh's call for independence for East Africa in 1950. This was the pre-condition for meeting the economic demands of working people.

At the same time, Makhan Singh realised that for both the struggles – economic and political – it was essential that people are politicised to understand the context of capitalism and imperialist rule, which the country was under. Liberation could not come if only a few people in trade unions and politics were aware of the social and political contradictions in the society. Years of colonial education and mass media propaganda from colonialism had influenced people's thinking along a 'colonial mind-set'. It was thus the entire population that had to be 'activated' by the provision of appropriate information and knowledge that were based on progressive, people-orientated ideas, values and experiences. Makhan Singh and the trade union movement that he led were active in various communication activities – including oral, pamphlets and newspapers.[51]

The Trade Union Movement Influences Mau Mau

Yet another area that many have ignored or dismissed is the influence of Makhan Singh and the trade union movement on Mau Mau, the national liberation movement. As we saw earlier, Makhan Singh was active in India in trade unions as well as in the struggle for independence from Britain. Similarly, he had these two aims in Kenya.

51 Further details of the communication activities of the trade union movement are available in Durrani (2006).

It is necessary to see the struggle for independence in its wider perspective. The role of the trade union movement and that of militant trade unionists such as Fred Kubai, Bildad Kaggia, Pio Gama Pinto and Makhan Singh in the achievement of independence has generally been sidelined in the history of Kenya, influenced by colonial and imperialist scholarship. They brought radical working class ideology, organisation and leadership to the national liberation struggle. This changed the politics of the time in a fundamental way. This revolutionary change was influenced in no small way by Makhan Singh and the militant trade union movement he helped create. The removal of the history of the trade union movement from the history and politics of Kenya's struggle for independence suits imperialism.

It is not that the contribution the militant, progressive trade union movement made to the struggle for independence is not well documented; it has been kept hidden in official records and history as taught in schools and colleges. It is thus not part of the national consciousness. A look at research and records on the contribution of the trade union movement to independence points the way to the need for further research on the topic. Newsinger (2006) explains these links, but he first sets the scene of the role played by Mau Mau:

> [Mau Mau] was without any doubt one of the most important revolutionary movements in the history of modern Africa and one of the most important revolutionary movements to confront the British Empire (p.186).

But the question then arises as to where the movement got its revolutionary agenda. That important input came from the trade union movement which itself was deeply influenced by the ideology and actions of Makhan Singh. Newsinger (2006) shows the radicalisation of the movement as coming from the trade union movement:

> The movement [Mau Mau] was radicalised by a militant leadership that emerged from the trade union movement in Nairobi. Here the Transport and Allied Workers Union led by Fred Kubai and the Clerks and Commercial Workers Union led by Bildad Kaggia were at the heart of the resistance. Most accounts of the Mau Mau movement either ignore or play down the role of the trade unions in the struggle, but the fact is that without their participation a sustained revolt would not have been possible (p. 186).

Bildad Kaggia joined the Labour Trade Union of East Africa (LTUEA), the general trade union set up by Makhan Singh when the union he tried to set up, the Clerks and Commercial Workers Union, could not be established. Later he became the president of the LUEA Kaggia (1975) looks at how the militant trade union movement entered the political arena and radicalised it:

> People in Nairobi looked to the trade unions for leadership, not to the 'political' leaders of KAU [Kenya African Union]. Encouraged by this support, the trade unions decided to try and capture the political leadership as well. We would begin by taking over the Nairobi branch of KAU.

Thus those involved in the radical trade union movement, including Makhan Singh, had a profound impact in the national liberation movement. Chandan (2015) confirms this:

> By the 1950s, new unions were forming, strikes were frequent and Makhan Singh directed trade unionism towards anti-colonial nationalist struggle, indeed the labour movement effectively turned into a militant vehicle for African political aspirations.

The full impact of Makhan Singh's contribution to the development of the radical Left in Kenya will ultimately emerge. Kinyatti (2008) hints at what is likely to emerge from such a fuller study:

> The EATUC leadership is credited with deepening the anti-imperialist resistance among the working class and for producing the Mau Mau revolutionary leadership. It is, therefore, important to note that the driving forces of the Mau Mau movement were the workers, the peasants and the patriotic petty-bourgeoisie. On every level of the struggle, the working class and its proletarian leadership played the leading role.

It is this history from a working class perspective that will finally restore Makhan Singh and other progressive, committed and socialist leaders and activists to their rightful place in the history of Kenya and in global anti-imperialist struggles.

Documenting Resistance

Documenting the history of resistance is an important role that liberation forces have to undertake so as to ensure that their version of history and events is not forgotten or seen from an enemy perspective. That was certainly the case with Makhan Singh who realised the importance of documenting workers' struggles so as to ensure that the current and future generation were not brought up on a blinkered version of history. For this, he left over 20,000 documents which are now in the Makhan Singh Archives at the University of Nairobi Library. Makhan Singh also wrote the two most important books on the history of Kenya: *History of Kenya's Trade Union Movement to 1952* (1969, Nairobi: East African Publishing House) and *Kenya's Trade Unions, 1952-56 Crucial Years* (ed. BA Ogot, 1980, Nairobi, Uzima Press). He was thus not only a prominent trade union organiser and a politician, but a historian who did much to preserve the working class history of Kenya. His political activism is indicated, for example, in the following extract from the Colonial Office files (Great Britain Colonial Office):

> Makhan published articles in the press, disseminated pamphlets and repeatedly addressed African audiences. He told them, inter alia, that His Majesty's Government was a 'foreign power who had no right to rule in Kenya', that the Kenya Government had introduced slavery, and that secret plans were being hatched to take more African land for the City of Nairobi.

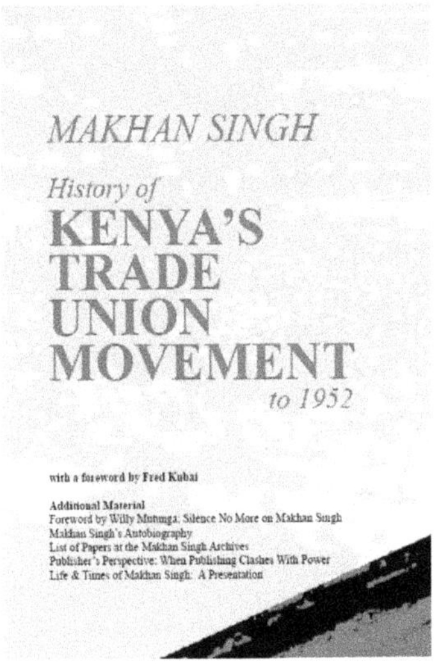

The leaflets issued during worker action provided valuable information for workers and were also a way of politicising workers to stand firm for their demands. Today, they provide historical records of an important period in Kenya's history. One such leaflet is reproduced hereunder:

5/4/1937. 126

Nairobi Workers Strike

OUR DEMANDS.

For the information of the general public and those concerned this is to notify that the demands of the workers who are on strike at various works are the following:

1 Eight hours day.
2 25 percent. increase in wages.
3 Recognisation of the Labour Trade Union of East Africa.
4 Taking back those workers who have struck.

Up till now the following employers have granted to their employers the above demands:

1 Tafail Mohamed, Contractor.
2 S. Nanak Singh, Furniture Maker.
3 Jagat Singh Bains, Contractor.
4 Karam Ali Nathoo, Box Body Maker.
5 Messrs. Thaker Singh & Co.,
6 Karam Chand, Furniture Maker.
7 N. B. Shah, Furniture Maker.

Makhan Singh,
Hon. Secretary,
The Labour Trade Union of E. A,

Nairobi, 5.4.37.

Khalsa Press, Nairobi.

It is a measure of the success of imperialism that such documents and historical records have been allowed to remain under-used on library shelves. But this also indicates that the message and the stand that Makhan Singh took has relevance even to this day as the ruling classes still fear his message captured in the foregoing terms — capitalist, workers, comrades, exploit, struggle, workers' rights. Again, this provides a strong indication for the working class and other struggling people in Kenya that their struggle has a legitimacy and a long history which they can draw upon for current and future battles. The examples that the militant trade unions under Makhan Singh and Mau Mau activists provided are aspects of Kenya's history that cannot be ignored or swept under the carpet. They continue to inform people's struggles not only in Kenya but in other parts of the world as well.

It is possible today to refer to the thousands of documents left by Makhan Singh to arrive at a working class history of Kenya and also to assess the role of trade unions and of Makhan Singh himself in their challenge to imperialism. What is lacking is an appropriate academic environment which can develop scholarship around working class history of Kenya. Perhaps a Kenyan university in the future will see it fit to set up a Trade Union and Liberation Research Institute to change people's perspectives on the liberation struggle on the role of trade unions in the struggle and also the role of pioneers such as Makhan Singh and others currently missing from national consciousness.

Conclusion

Imperialism has a short-term perspective on people's resistance to its domination over people's rights and resources. Its interest is to maximum power, profits and control. Its approach is that the long-term would take care of itself — assuming the world survives the environmental degradation created by capitalism. On the other hand, those who resist imperialism, of necessity, have to have a long term perspective on their struggles, their sacrifices and their victories. Each battle lost provides lessons for the next battle; each victory strengthens the prospects for the final victory.

Thus imperialist defeat in Vietnam is easily forgotten amidst the euphoria of current victories of globalisation and new conquests globally. Mao Zedong, Ho Chi Minh, Fidel Castro, Kwame Nkrumah, Patrice Lumumba, Dedan Kimathi, among many others, are turned into villains and best forgotten according to imperialism. To this way of thinking, Makhan Singh is but a passing phase, easily disregarded and whose memory is sealed in dusty archives. Pio Gama Pinto matters little; Mau Mau has but little interest in the comprador-controlled Kenya after independence.

But people who struggle, who resist, who lose lives, land and freedom forget little. The surface may be calm. But deep waves run under the calm surface. Makhan Singh is dead, but his revolutionary legacy cannot die. It will arise from the depths as a deadly tsunami to take charge of the next wave of resistance and struggle. That is the lasting – and perhaps the best – testimonial for Makhan Singh and heroes like him.

People like Makhan Singh never expect any rewards. They do selfless service to whatever cause they passionately believe in, then quietly depart, leaving a great mark behind, says Hindpal Jabbal. The mark that Makhan Singh has left can never be erased.

References

Chandan, Amarjit (2015): 'Gopal Singh: an account of an EA Trade Unionist'. in Durrani, Shiraz (ed.): *Makhan Singh: A revolutionary Kenyan trade unionist.*

Durrani, Shiraz (2006): *Never Be Silent: Publishing and Imperialism in Kenya, 1884-1963.* Nairobi: Vita Books.

Durrani, Shiraz (ed. 2015): *Makhan Singh, A Revolutionary Kenyan Trade Unionist.* Nairobi: Vita Books.

Great Britain. Colonial Office files: 'Case History of Makhan Singh'. Provided by Amarjit Chandan from the National Archive Kew, England. 2014. SC (61)33.

Jabbal, Hindpal (2015): 'My Father, Makhan Singh'. in Durrani, Shiraz (ED., 2015): *Makhan Singh, A Revolutionary Kenyan Trade Unionist.* Nairobi: Vita Books.

Kaggia, Bildad (1975): *Roots of Freedom, 1921-1963: The Autobiography of Bildad Kaggia.* Nairobi: East African Publishing House.

Kasrils, Ronnie (2013): 'How the ANC's Faustian pact sold out South Africa's poorest: In the early 1990s, we in the leadership of the ANC made a serious error. Our people still paying the price.' *The Guardian.* 24 June 2013. Available at: http://m.guardian.co.uk/commentisfree/2013/jun/24/anc-faustian-pact-mandela-fatal-error [Accessed: 30-06-13].

Kenya, Colony and Protectorate (1961). Governor's Office. Makhan

Singh (1961). FCO 141/6870. File No. GO/POL/2/27/. Extracts from the minutes of the 77th Meeting of the Council of Ministers held on 18th October 1961. 1056. The Deportation (Immigrant British Subjects Ordinance, 1949. Makhan Singh.

Kinyatti, Maina (2008): *History of resistance in Kenya, 1884-2002.* Nairobi: Mau Mau Research Centre.

Kubai, Fred (1969): 'Foreword' to Singh, Makhan (1969): *History of Kenya's trade union movement to 1952.* Nairobi: East African Publishing House.

Milne, Seumas (2013): 'Egypt, Brazil, Turkey: without politics, protest is at the mercy of the elites.' *The Guardian.* Available at: http://m.guardian.co.uk/commentisfree/2013/jul/02/politics-protest-elites-brazil-egypt-organisation?CMP=EMCNEWEML6619I2 [Accessed: 03-07-13].

Newsinger, John (2006): *The Blood Never Dried: A people's history of the British Empire.* London: Bookmarks.

Ogot, Bethwell A (1980): 'Introduction.' Singh, Makhan (1980).

Ouma, Steve and Makau Mutua (2006): 'Foreword.' Patel, Zarina (2006): *Unquiet, the life and times of Makhan Singh.* Nairobi: Zand Graphics.

Patel, Zarina (2006): *Unquiet: the life and times of Makhan Singh.* Nairobi: Zand graphics.

Seidenberg, Dana April (1983): *Uhuru and the Kenya Indians: the role of a minority community in Kenya politics, 1939-1963.* New Delhi: Vikas.

Sicherman, Carol. (1990): *Ngugi wa Thiong'o: The making of a rebel: a source book in Kenyan literature and resistance.* London: Hans Zell. (Documentary Research in African Literature, 1).

Singh, Makhan (1963): 'Comrade Makhan Singh.' in Patel, Ambu H. (Compiler, 1963): *Struggle for Release of Jomo & His Colleagues.* Nairobi: New Kenya Publishers. pp. 141-150. The autobiography is written in the third person. It is reproduced in this book.

Singh, Makhan (1969): *History of Kenya's Trade Union Movement to 1952.* Nairobi: East African Publishing House. Singh, Makhan

Singh, Makhan (1980): *Kenya's Trade Unions: Crucial years, 1952-56.* Nairobi: Uzima Press.

Kenya's Colonisation Prepared the Country for Exploitation

Saleh Mamon[52]

By any account, the 1920s were years of turmoil internationally. Kenya was not isolated. It was dragged through mud and blood by British colonialism, which tore up the fabric of the existing society across the land by destroying any resistance to dispossession of land by every community that stood up to fight when the construction of the railway began in Mombasa in 1896 and reached deep into the interior within six years. Build by Indian indentured labour, the railway was to change Kenya forever.

Land Grab by White Settlers with State Assistance

The railway laid Kenya open to world trade and exploitation. The preconditions were the land grabbed from Africans be given cheaply to white settlers and to use administrative measures to forcibly procure wage labourers. The Crown Lands Ordinance of 1915 transferred millions of acres of African land to the ownership of Europeans and vetoed any land transaction involving people of non-European descent, including Africans. The land seized was handed over to White setters, speculators, military personnel, military veterans, merchants, bankers and big capitalist farmers.

Africans Reduced to A Servant Class

Africans were restricted to designated reserves, which had less fertile soil. Hut tax and poll tax were imposed on adults. Masters and servants legislation was first adopted in Kenya in 1906. The law was used as a weapon for disciplining labour, allowing extra-judicial beatings to be administered in the workplace. Casual labour was incentivised so that it could combine with African agricultural work. Men cooked for

52 Saleh Mamon was born in Meru, Kenya. He completed his secondary education at Eastleigh Secondary School and Jamhuri High School, Nairobi, where he was a awarded a Kenya Teacher's Scholarship to Edinburgh University to read biological science. After qualifying he returned to Kenya to teach biology at Eastleigh Secondary for five years. He returned to the United Kingdom to teach secondary science, obtained two post graduate degrees, an M.Sc. and M.Ed. (London) and retired as a headteacher. He passed away after a long illness as this book was in pre-publication preparation.

European settlers, tended European livestock, milked dairy cattle, and marketed the produce. Women and juveniles were drawn into daily casual labour on farms. Earning a wage to survive and pay colonial taxes became a general necessity.

African Labour Capture

By the 1920s, the control of the movement of labour became entrenched. All African males above the age of 15 had to carry an identity document, the *kipande*, around their neck: it had personal details, fingerprints, and an employment history. Africans were forbidden to travel in certain areas, to sleep in certain areas, to accept employment or to bring their families from rural areas to urban centres without colonial authorisation. The *kipande* became hated by all Africans.

Growth of Commodity Market: Kenya Enters the World Market

Soon the most fertile lands were under monoculture to produce tea, coffee, sisal, etc. to serve the metropolitan British economy. The interior opened to commerce through the immigration of the Indian traders, artisans, and builders. The *dukawallah* (shopkeepers) in towns became the nodal points of commodity exchange purchasing native produce through cash, which the natives used to buy all their necessities from clothes, blankets, to kerosene etc. The cash nexus developed rapidly. Villages grew into townships and towns into small cities. The Kenyan economy thus became integrated, however unevenly, into the world market.

Armed Africans Used for Policing

Each district town would have a District Commissioner's office with a prison and district court. Policing was by the Askari, a class of recruited African soldier. This class was trained to be loyal to the colonial authority and willing to maintain the status quo by shooting to kill Africans. They could be mobilised to form garrisons or internal security forces when necessary. At the apex was the totalitarian governor-general exercising power through decrees and often states of emergency, with a token legislative assembly.

German and British Bring along Attrition in East Africa 1914 to 1918

Kenya was not isolated from explosive international developments. The rival British and German powers were engaged in a long war of attrition across the Kenya-Tanganyika border as well as the Malawi border further south. Nearly 200,000 Africans were recruited into the British army, with one fourth losing their lives. The war devastated an area five times the size of Germany and lasted much longer than the one in Europe, with civilian suffering on a scale unimaginable in Europe.

Lenin's Clarion Call for Liberation in the Colonial World

At the end of the the First World War, there was revolutionary agitation across Europe. The Russian revolution of October 17 shook the world. Soon after, Lenin issued a clarion call to colonial subjects dominated by the British/French and other colonial powers to liberate themselves. The colonial powers launched a counter-revolution in response by intervening in the Russian civil war and made efforts to counter any revolutionary and communist tendencies both at home and in the colonies.

British Suppress Any Ghadar Revolutionary Party

The British authorities used draconian measures to suppress any liberation movement. A good example is the suppression of the Ghadar(Revolution) Party, which was founded in 1913 in the USA by Sikh immigrants who went to work in the fields, factories, and logging camps of Northern California and the Pacific Northwest around Sacramento. In a short period, it became a worldwide revolutionary formation. It soon had 10,000 members and established branches across the world: groups existed in Afghanistan, China, India and elsewhere; its multi-lingual weekly, *The Ghadar*, had readers in Egypt, Madagascar, Morocco, Reunion, South Africa, Sudan and Kenya.

It was influenced in its early days by anarchism and syndicalism. Its aim was to rid India of British colonialism and to establish a new egalitarian non-hierarchical social order. Members of the party were detained, deported or hanged for mere possession of the party newspaper. With the onset of the First World War, the British Government carried out mass arrests and executions of the Ghadarites in all its colonies. No trials were held. In British East Africa (re-named Kenya in 1920), the Ghadarites were charged with sedition – three were shot, two were hanged, eight were imprisoned and about 20 were deported to India. During 1915 and 1916, at least 400 Ghadar members were hanged. Three Punjabis, Bishan Singh of village Gakhal Jalandhar, as well as Ganesh Das and Yog Raj Bali of Rawalpindi, were summarily tried and hanged in public in December 1915 for possessing and distributing *Ghadar*. In spite of this, members of the Ghadar party worked clandestinely across East Africa in all fields including trade unions until the 1940s.

Counter-revolution Follows the Russian Revolution

The Russian revolution immediately led to counter revolutionary measures by the Imperial powers in Europe. Nearly 17 armies landed in the north of Russia to intervene in the Russian civll war on the side of the counter revolutionaries in an attempt to destroy the revolution. It also meant suppression of any rebellion at home in European countries, the USA and in the colonies.

The British rulers in India were terrified by the idea of the spread of communism. There was a series of conspiracy plots that the British administration alleged leading to the imprisonment of political activists. The Peshawar Conspiracy trials involved five cases running from 1922 to 1927 against migrants who allegedly sneaked into India from Russia to start a communist movement. In the Kanpur Bolshevik Case in 1924, the newly emerged communists of India MN Roy, Muzaffar Ahmed, SA Dange, Shaukat Usmani, Nalini Gupta, Singaravelu Chettiar and Ghulam Hussain were arrested for conspiring against the colonial government. The accused were charged with trying "to deprive the King Emperor of his sovereignty of British India by complete separation of India from imperialistic Britain by a violent revolution." Perhaps the most well-known of all the communist plot cases brought by the British government was the Meerut conspiracy case of 1929. This had enormous political importance for the working class movement in India, where 31 labour leaders, including three Englishmen, were detained on conspiracy charges.

Massacres Follow

It is in this light that one should view the massacres that were to follow. On April 13, 1919, a large peaceful unarmed crowd gathered at Jallianwala Bagh in Amritsar to protest against the arrest of their leaders under the draconian Rowlatt Act, which sought to curb any revolutionary upsurge through arrest, and indefinite detention without trial or judicial review. Jallianwala could only be exited on one side as its other three sides were enclosed by buildings. After blocking the only exit, General Dyer ordered his troops to shoot at the crowd. The troops continued to fire till their ammunition was exhausted. Estimates vary but nearly 1,500 or more were killed, and 1,200 injured.

Destroying the Communist 'Menace'

Countering the communist menace became the top priority for the coming decades only to intensify during the Cold War with the rise of McCarthyism in America. Communist parties were targeted for destruction across the Third World. Bringing an end to Soviet communism was a key aim. All revolutionary movements across the world were to be opposed. Individual communists were incarcerated or assassinated. It was a perilous world for revolutionaries.

Meanwhile India, during the political ferment of the 1920, saw the emergence of revolutionaries like Bhagat Singh who along with his comrades Sukhdev and Rajguru, was hanged by the colonial regime on March 23, 1931. The trial of the three young revolutionaries was one of the finest moments in the freedom struggle of India. They used the opportunity of the trial to highlight the oppressive nature of British rule. A deep thinker, Bhagat Singh had extensively studied socialism, marxism and history. His death led to a new national awakening with his photograph on sale in every city and town.

The Young Kikuyu Association -- First Anti-imperialist Movement

Back in Kenya, the Young Kikuyu Association (YKA) was founded by Harry Thuku as the first anti-imperialist movement in June 1921 in Pangani, Nairobi. It organised mass rallies against the *kipande* system, forced labour policies, sexual assaults on African women by white settlers, racial segregation, the expropriation of land and the system of taxation. It demanded the establishment of a democratic system and equal distribution of the nation's wealth. Within a very short time, a large force of African working class people joined the association. The YKA formed an alliance with progressive Indian political organisations, groups and individuals.

By July 1921, the YKA dissolved and upgraded to a nationwide and regional nationalist anti-colonialist movement, the East African Association (EAA). The EAA built international links with WEB Du Bois' National Association for the Advancement of Coloured People (NAACP) and Marcus Garvey's the Universal Negro Improvement Association (UNIA). At the second Pan African Congress in London in 1921, two Indian members AM Jeevanjee and Varma represented the EAA. The EAA adopted a manifesto with 14 demands.

The colonial government was heavily opposed to the aims and activities of the EAA and moved to ban it. Harry Thuku was arrested on March 14, 1922 in connection with his political activities with two of his co-leaders, Waiganjo wa Ndotono and George Mugekenyi.

On March 16, a crowd of 7,000 to 8,000 marched to the police headquarters. The police opened fire on unarmed protestors. Fleeing protestors were also fired upon by white settlers and game hunters at the nearby Norfolk Hotel. Some 250 protestors were shot dead and hundreds were seriously injured. Muthoni wa Nyanjiru and Macaria wa Kiboi, two leaders of the protest, were martyred. Mass arrests and imprisonment followed to terrorise the people. Thuku was exiled to Kismayu in Somalia.

The first general strike in Kenya was triggered as a protest against the arrest of Harry Thuku and the killings of the protestors. The workers' demands included the nationalist demands of the EAA. These were the abolition of the *kipande* system and forced labour, the improvement of wages and working conditions, the reduction of taxes, the return of African lands, improvement of education and the election of Africans to the Legislative Council.

Makhan Singh Enters Kenya

Makhan Singh opened the 'proverbial trapdoor' to enter the world in Kenya after travelling from India at the age of 14. The two worlds were connected historically by British colonisation. There are many differences between the two worlds. British colonisation of India started around 1750 and was entering the late phase of massive agitation for independence. The colonisation of Kenya was accelerated. One reason for that was to set up a White settler colony rapidly and integrate the country with the British economy.

During the period of his schooling in Nairobi, Makhan Singh continued taking interest in world events and was influenced by the workers' and peasants' movements (both communist and socialist) and trade union struggles. At the same time, he also commenced composing and reciting poems in Punjabi on religious, social and political subjects with emphasis on the struggle for freedom. When he started to work at his father's printing press in 1931, he had opportunities to continue serious study of political literature of all types. He had access to documents which enabled him to link with the various communist organisations in South Africa, Britain and India. As mentioned earlier, Kenya had an early taste of anti-imperialist movements in the Ghadar movement when its members were hanged, detained or deported. He developed his thinking on the historical position of these organisations, his own links and his politics.

Early Resistance of Workers in East Africa

In his later life, Makhan Singh researched and documented workers' resistance to Portuguese and British colonialism against the conditions they worked under. Workers often revolted spontaneously when they faced injustice. Some notable strikes were: Railway workers (1900); Police constables (1902); workers on government farms (1908); railway Indian workers at Kilindini harbour (1908); rickshaw pullers in Nairobi (1908); African boat workers in Mombasa (1912); Railway goods shed workers in Nairobi (1912); and African workers on settlers' farms (1912). Besides these, there were general strikes in 1922, 1939, 1947 and 1950.

Workers formed associations for collective action to address common grievances and seek protection against employers picking them out. Examples of such activism are: Indian Trade Union Mombasa (1914); the Railway Artisan Union (1922); the Trade Union Committee of Mombasa (1922); the Workers Protective Society of Kenya (1931); and the Indian Trade Union(1933), which later changed its name to Kenya Indian Labour Trade Union. Notice how confined these are within communities and traditional boundaries.

Obstacles to Workers Organisations

At that time, industry was relatively undeveloped. Railways was an exception. Ports were developing. Employment was precarious and contracts short term. A worker was compelled to go from job to job, workshop to workshop, town to town. Makhan Singh identified all the factors that affected trade unions.

There was no trade union legislation protecting workers, and existing legislation discouraged the formation of trade unions. Organisers faced the general hostility of employers and colonial officials. The threat of victimisation by employers and or/deportation by the colonial government was always present.

All this was compounded by the absence of workers who, after being elected officials of the union, were prepared to devote their time regularly and fearlessly to making the union function in a spirit of cooperation, unity, sacrifice and service.

Breaking the Stasis

Makhan Singh broke this stasis. Being part of the workers organised in the printing press must have provided the opportunities for him to understand the challenges faced by the workers in terms of pay and conditions. Most of all this practical experience in presswork was invaluable when he need to use various methods of communication such as handbills, leaflets, newspapers, organising meetings, making speeches, using creative poetry to convey to the workers the class nature of their struggle in Kenya.

His politics come through in the lexicon he used. Gone is the language of patronage between the bosses and workers, the deference. Instead, there is emphasis on the class struggle between capitalists and workers. A good example is the leaflet, printed in November 1936, in support of the workers of the firm M/s Karsan Ladha who went on strike for higher wages.

Under the title 'Struggle Between Capitalists and Workers has Started in Earnest', it urges "Our worker comrades! Come forward! March ahead! If you do not march ahead today, then remember that you will be crushed under the heels of capitalists tomorrow. Workers should have a united stand and should stand up strongly against the capitalists so that they should not ever have the courage to attempt and exploit workers again, nor to take away workers' rights from them".

This is a militant assertive call. It is a departure from the way workers fought for their rights in the colonial period. The paradigm shift with terms such as capitalist, workers, comrades, exploit, struggle and worker' rights shows a revolutionary with advanced consciousness and a remarkable grasp of Marxian theory of class struggle.

A Life-long Communist

It seems that Makhan Singh developed an unshakeable life-long conviction politically that he was a communist dedicated to the advancement of the working class. He shared this with the founders of modern socialism, Marx and Engels, who right till the end of their lives continued to believe in the historical mission of the working class to free society from capitalist exploitation. At some point, Makhan Singh joined the Indian Communist Party.

Remarkable Ability to Organise Workers

It is clear that he had an immense capacity for organising workers using every means possible such as holding meetings, distributing handouts, publishing newsletters, speaking at public meetings and negotiating with employers. This meant organising and chairing the trade union internally with the regular meetings of the central committee and other committee.

Planning a successful strike also was not an easy matter. Giving employers notice of strikes, negotiating, organising strike committees, providing food for strikers, keeping morale up during a strike, and holding rallies require a lot of energy and skills.

Organising Trade Unions – Breaching Racial Boundaries
It is this dedication to organising that led to Makhan Singh being elected as Secretary of Indian Trade Union (ITU) in 1935 at the age of 22. Holding such an executive position enabled him to influence the future direction of the ITU. He convinced his nearly 500 fellow trade unionists to be open to all workers irrespective of race, religion and colour by changing their name to Labour Trade Union of Kenya (LTUK) indicating his intention to break free from the racial and political narrowness of daily life in Kenya.

By 1937 LTUK expanded its geographical reach by becoming the Labour Trade Union of East Africa (LTUEA). Becoming more plural and inclusive across three colonial countries was a highly progressive move.

At its third conference, two prominent Africans, Jesse Kariuki and George Ndegwa were elected to the Executive Committee of the union, the first as Vice-President and the second as member of the Committee.

These steps were revolutionary as they breached the colonial strategy and tactics of keeping the working class divided by race or locality.

Showing Practical Genius at Organising
Makhan Singh showed his genius as an organiser. Under his guidance, the LTUK swiftly began to function as an organisation. An office was rented and furnished with the necessary equipment like a typewriter and a rotary cyclostyling machine set to work. A cycle of meetings of the management committee and constitutional sub-committee was put in place. A drive to enrol members commenced.

Marx wrote in *Capital* Volume I: "Hence in the history of capitalist production, the determination of the working day presents itself as the result of a struggle, a struggle between collective capital, i.e., the class of capitalists, and collective labour, i.e., the working class." As a purchaser of labour power of a worker, the capitalist tries to make the working-day as long as possible without regard to the health and well being of the worker to extract as much surplus labour from the worker. This struggle in England led to The Factory Act of 1850, which limited the average working-day to 10 hours in 1867.

In 1830s, long working days became a major grievance as well. On August 10, 1935, a resolution was passed by a mass meeting of LTUK which condemned the actions of those employers who were weakening workers physically and demanded that all employers should limit the working day to no more than eight hours without a diminution of wages.

This campaign was the most popular of all. It was promoted through handbills, meetings in residential areas, works-discussions and public announcements (preceded by ringing of a large bell in the main thoroughfares of Nairobi. After about 10 days of campaigning, daily mass meeting began to be held in the Ramgharia Plot, Campos Ribeiro Avenue, to further the demand. The campaign created a more militant spirit among the union workers.

The employers acceded to the demands. The effects of the success was felt all over Kenya and in Uganda and Tanzania, too. African workers supported and joined the union, whose membership increased to more than 1,000.

Striking for Wage Increases

The capitalist class always suppresses wages because wages and profits are inversely related -- the lower the wages the greater the profits. The working class is always contending to maintain its living standards against price increases in basic necessities, rents, etc. In 1937, the LTUK was confident enough to mobilise workers to bid for wage increases.

It planned to go on a complete strike from April 1, 1937. Notice was issued to the employers. A strike committee was formed. Picketing was organised at all the workplaces. A free kitchen was set up for the strikers and the unemployed to have their daily food.

The employers resisted these wage demands. After 62 days, they relented and agreed in writing to wage increases of 15 to 22 per cent, an eight-hour day, and reinstatement of all the strikers.
The Great Depression, starting from the 1929 Wall Street Crash, had affected both richer and poor countries, eroding standards of living. This was a great achievement. Union membership rose to about 2,500.

Trade Union Legislation

Realising that the trade union movement in Kenya had come to stay, the government published a Trade Union Bill in the middle of 1937 when the strike was still continuing. It became an Ordinance in August. LTUK was registered under it in September 1937. This brought to an end the historical period when unions were banned and illegal -- at least for this moment. It did not mean that the colonial state would not move against the unions in future, banning strikes, etc.

Linking the Economic to the Political

Workers organising to earn better wages in the workplace would generally wish to confine their struggle to their workplace. Capitalist employers would rather have no unions but once there are unions, they would like to limit their influence. They are inclined to believe in the working of the market and would like their workers to be apolitical.

At the same time, the capitalist class ensures that they control the government which has the power to raise taxes, control money supply, maintain law and order, guarantee property rights, pass laws to control strikes, etc. This they do through political parties winning elections and forming governments. Most such parties are business-leaning and the working class rarely have a party that controls the state. Nonetheless, working class votes are important and their loyalties are won by promises of jobs, housing, etc.

Makhan Singh's important contribution to the liberation struggle in Kenya was to link the economic struggle to the political struggle. For him it was essential to win political power to satisfy the economic demands of the working people so that society could be reorganised to bring prosperity to workers and the people of Kenya. Practical issues from housing, wages, working conditions, health and safety, education, etc would require legislation to ensure investment, set standards and ensure accountability. Trade unions would be centres of democracy, ensuring the democracy is exercised in local and central government.

By 1938, Makhan Singh became an active member of the East African Indian National Congress, becoming a member of Congress Standing and Executive Committees and campaigning on issues of racial discrimination and the White Highlands.

Working with the Youth

In 1939, Makhan Singh was appointed Secretary of the Indian Youth League, which had previously played an important role in shortening the working hours of shop assistants. It was now active in encouraging the activities of gymnasiums and adult education.

After his arrival back in Kenya, in December 1947, he was one of the active organisers of the Kenya Youth Conference and was elected one of its three vice-presidents.

Travel Back to India

In June 1939, Makhan Singh had requested the LTUEA for leave to visit India for a few months and this was granted in December. He expressly stated that he was taking temporary leave and left Gopal Singh Chandan in charge of the LTUEA. The purpose of the visit was for family reasons as well as to study working class conditions and trade union activities in Bombay and Ahmedabad.

Makhan Singh sailed from Mombasa on Thursday, December 28, 1939. The steamer stopped at Seychelles and Goa before reaching Bombay on January 6, 1940. Before disembarking he disguised himself as a Muslim. He shaved off his beard and long hair (kesh), put on a Muslim cap and wrapped a tehmet (sarong) around his waist.

He had good reason to be cautious, even in India. Late in 1939, Mota Singh, a former president of the LTUEA and one of the very active communists of his time, was arrested again in India in 1939. He was tortured in the infamous Lahore Shahi Qila (fort) and remained in prison until 1945.

The government's disapproval of trade unions in general and its hostility to Makhan Singh, the general secretary of the LTUEA, were unmistakable. On January 5, 1940, the acting attorney-general had, during a debate, informed the Legco (Legislative Council) that the secretary of the union had left for India. One member asked rhetorically if he too could be imprisoned for subversive activities.

Makhan Singh was well aware that he too could be arrested. Hence the disguise, but his activist spirit would not allow him to remain idle, even in hiding. In Bombay, he attended the popularly anticipated 'Independence Day' celebrations, which were held on January 26.

He threw himself in India's freedom struggle and participated in the Independence Day celebrations on January 26, 1940. He got in touch with underground comrades and was assigned to work in Ahmedabad, a large industrial city, 500 kilometres north of Bombay.

He travelled there exactly a month later and began working with a textile union. February 1940 was taken up by organising strike actions with the textile workers demanding not only better wages and conditions of work, but also 'swaraj' or full independence.

In the first week of March, Makhan Singh addressed a large mass meeting of about 30,000 workers and strikers and, later in the month, attended a Ramgharia session of the Indian National Congress as a fraternal delegate from East Africa.

It was in this session that Congress gave full authority to Mahatma Gandhi to launch a Satyagraha movement whenever he deemed it necessary. On May 1, 1940, Makhan Singh participated in a May Day parade.

With the intensification of the freedom-struggle and working class movement, the imperialist rulers began arresting and detaining prominent leaders and workers throughout India.

On May 5, 1940, Makhan Singh was arrested at Ahmedabad on the orders of the Central Government and detained in the historic Sabarmati Jail. No charges were brought against him and he was moved to different locations of detention: Lahore Fort, Mazaffargarh Jail, Deoli Detention Camp, and Gujarat Jail.

During his detention, he came into contact with communist, socialist, and other revolutionary leaders from all over India.

From October to November 1941, he was on hunger strike along with more than 160 other detainees in Deoli Detention Camp over the conditions under which they were kept, which were radically improved thereafter.

Makhan Singh was released from detention in July 1942 and immediately thereafter, an internment order was served upon him restricting him to the limits of the village of Gharjakh where he was born.

He remained under restriction until he was unconditionally released on January 18, 1945. Thus he remained under detention and restriction in India for about four-and-a-half years.

He then began working as a sub-editor of *Jang-I-Azadi*, the weekly organ of the Panjab Committee of the Communist Party of India, and continued in the role up to the end of July 1947. One of the main aims of Makhan Singh's life, the freedom of India, having been achieved, he left for Kenya in the first week of August 1947.

Return to Kenya and Facing Deportation Orders Twice

Makhan Singh arrived in Nairobi on August 22, 1947. Five days later, a quit-order was served upon him by the government of Kenya asking him to leave Kenya within 30 days as, according to the government, he had previously, in May 1947, been declared a prohibited immigrant and had been allowed to enter Kenya by "oversight"

He refused to obey the order and was prosecuted. The court acquitted him and the government could not deport him. No official reason was given for its action against him. It was revealed in the House of Commons that Makhan Singh had been declared a prohibited immigrant on account of his activities when he was previously in Kenya.

On October 5, 1948, he was arrested for the second time on a warrant for deportation on the grounds that he was a prohibited immigrant. He was tried by the Supreme Court, which ruled that he could not be deported because he was a permanent resident of Kenya. He was set free within two weeks of his arrest.

He had to wait 16 years to be granted a certificate of Permanent Residence in 1967.

Activities with East African Indian National Congress

From 1947 to 1952, all trade union activities were proscribed in Kenya. Makhan Singh worked behind the scenes with prominent black trade unionists — Bildad Kaggia, Aggrey Minya and Tom Mboya.

Makhan Singh became active in the East African Indian National Congress. He was a leading campaigner during the May 1948 Legco elections when Congress put up its own candidates.

In June 1948, he went on a fast to protest against the government policy of dividing the Indian voters roll on religious grounds and against the policies of communal leaders.

In August 1948, he was elected to the Standing and Executive Committees of the Congress.

Cost of Living and Wages Conference

In September 1948, Makhan Singh called this conference as General Secretary of the Labour Trade Union of East Africa.

It was attended by representatives of several unions. The main significance of the conference was that African and Asian trade unionists met together independently of the Labour Department to discuss burning questions and decided to act together in future.

East African Trade Union Congress

Makhan Singh with other African and Asian trade unionists set up the EATUC in 1949 with Fred Kubai as the President, while Makhan became its General Secretary. The Congress helped in coordinating the activities of trade unionists and in conducting the joint struggle of African and Asian workers for better conditions of employment.

Makhan Singh's Resolution and Call for Complete Independence

On April 23, 1950 a mammoth mass meeting was held in the Kaloleni Hall, Nairobi, under the joint auspices of Kenya African Union (KAU) and East African Indian National Congress (EAINC).

The meeting was in response to the so-called Kenya Plan championed by the European Electors' Union for the establishment of a British East Dominion similar to the white dominion of Canada, Australia and New Zealand, which were self governing colonies dealing with all internal matters -- with their own Parliament as an independent member of the British Commonwealth. For the White settlers of Kenya, an entity similar to the Union of South Africa with a Parliament consisting of a senate and a House of Assembly was an attractive proposition.

Makhan Singh boldly took the floor to move an addendum to the resolution about the constitutional changes in Tanganyika declaring that "the real solution", which should be implemented "at an early" date, had to be "the complete independence and sovereignty of the East African territories".

In an impassioned speech, he asserted that time had come for the people to unite and demand in a single voice that the country was theirs and no foreign power had the right to rule over it. In his view, that should be the aim of Africans, Indians and progressive Europeans.

Since, the British Government had recently declared independence of India, Burma and Ceylon, it should similarly do likewise for the East African territories.

One ought not to underestimate the importance of this move politically. This was the first time in the history of East Africa when a resolution on complete independence was proposed and adopted. It did upset the colonial authorities much.

Makhan did not remain quiet on this issue because he believed that the demands of working people could only be met once they won political power to make appropriate policies unencumbered by corporate and financial capitalist interests. On May Day, he wrote: "The call of May Day 1950 in the middle of the twentieth century is that the workers and the peoples of of East Africa, should further strengthen their unity, should become more resolute and thus speed up the movement for freedom of all workers and peoples of East Africa".

In the evening to celebrate May Day, representatives of all trade unions met under the auspices of the East African Trade Union Congress. They pledged to build a strong trade union movement and to fully support the KAU and EAINC in carrying out the resolution of complete independence for the East African territories.

The State of Emergency and Mau Mau Uprising

While Makhan Singh was incarcerated, a cataclysm broke over Kenya which traumatised the whole society.

Although the Mau Mau wore the moniker framed by the colonial security establishment proudly, it did mystify their original goal expressed as the Land and Freedom Army. They demanded that their land taken from them during colonisation be returned to the rightful owners.

They were one of the most revolutionary movements to challenge the might of the British Empire in Africa at the same time as the Algerian Revolution was under way. The driving force of the movement were the workers, squatters, peasants and the patriotic petty-bourgeoisie.

They were radicalised by a militant leadership that emerged from the trade union movement in Nairobi. At the heart of resistance were the Transport and Allied Workers Union led by Fred Kubai and the Clerks and Commercial Workers Union led by Bildad Kaggia.

By the 1950s, new unions were forming, inspired by the Makhan Singh's successes in mobilising the LTUK for the eight-hour workday campaign and then winning wage rises for the LTUEA. The Labour movement had been converted into a militant movement for national liberation.

The Mau Mau set up its Central Committee. They began organising their congresses in the forest to discuss strategies, war plans and opening up five fronts. They organised the first Kenyan Parliament.

Jomo Kenyatta, president of the KAU, was arrested and charged with managing the Mau Mau, a secret society. He was flown to a remote location and held incommunicado. During Operation Jock Scott, 180 alleged nationalist leaders were arrested and sent to a concentration camp in Kajiado to be interrogated and tortured. They included administrators of independent schools, churches, teachers, pastors and students.

Mau Mau hardly had any modern weapons. The light arms they had, such as rifles and pistols, were often locally made. Their supplies often came from raiding arms depositories of the government. They set up supply lines, intelligence gathering lines, recruited administrative cadres, and set up bases in the forests.

The supply lines, from the supporters to the fighters, were through a network in Nairobi and other towns. That is why the security services sealed off Nairobi during Operation Anvil in 1954. All African adult men were stopped and searched. Nearly 50,000 Africans were screened and almost 24,000 were transported in special war trains to concentration camps.

Over the course of the emergency period, hanging judges traversed the country, carrying out summary hangings of 1,090 Kikuyus. Jomo Kenyatta was sentenced to seven years of imprisonment with hard labour along with Bildad Kaggia, Fred Kubai, and others. Pio Gama Pinto, editor-in -chief of the pro-Mau Mau paper, *The High Command,* was imprisoned without trial.

The counter-terrorism during the State of Emergency from September 1952 was a thousand times more violent. No black African, especially Kikuyu, was safe. The entire Kikuyu community was suspect. Stop and search was widespread. Shoot to kill was the operational policy. Murder and rape, beatings and humiliation were choice weapons of the local loyalists.

The adults were rounded up and interrogated at screening centres across the country. Individuals were classified as white, grey or black. 'Whites' were co-operative detainees released to the reserves, 'Greys' had taken oaths and the more compliant were detained to work in camps, 'Blacks' were hard core and imprisoned in detention camps. An elaborate pipeline to sort these was set up across the country. Torture in secrecy was widespread to obtain confessions.

The whole Kikuyu community was moved into protected villages which were fenced and put under surveillance with home guards on watch towers. There was immense privation with poor food supply.

The British army battalions were deployed against guerrillas in the forests. Modern aircraft were used to destroy KLFA positions. The British army launched major operations against the KLFA in the forests. The KLFA faced defeat against the overwhelming British fire power on many fronts.

The colonial government also turned the struggle for freedom into a civil war. Kikuyus loyal to the British were rewarded. Armed home guards who kept watch over the community were rewarded. Armed black soldiers were deployed against the land and freedom army.

Newspapers, magazines, documentaries, and feature films were used to demonise the Mau Mau as diseased minds, savages, satanic, etc. The propaganda disseminated across the entire society through radio, schools, churches, cinemas was very powerful. Their narrative could not be challenged.

The number of deaths during the emergency is a very contentious subject. Most are estimates and the issue is unlikely to be settled. By the end of the emergency period over four years, some 63 European civilians had died at the hands of the Mau Mau and 1,800 African civilians. Over 10,000 Mau Mau died. The Kenya Human Rights Commission has recently alleged that 90,000 Kenyans were executed, tortured or maimed during the crackdown, and that 160,000 people were detained in poor conditions. One estimate put the deaths of Kikuyus as high as 300,000.

The uprising came to an end when Dedan Kimathi, the Commander in Chief of the KLFA was wounded and captured on October 21, 1956. He was brought to trial and found guilty. He was sentenced to death and hanged in Nairobi on February 18, 1957. He did not ask for mercy from the court and told the court that if the court allowed, he was willing to negotiate the departure of the British from Kenya.

The aim of the colonial government was to ensure that the White settlers retained their land. If they could not have a settler state, then they could have the next best option — a black conservative government which would safeguard British interests and the land occupied by the settlers.

Makhan Singh's Release on the Eve of Independence

On the day of his release, Makhan Singh openly declared that he was still a communist and would continue his political and trade union activities. He added: "The duty of all freedom loving peoples of Kenya is to unite under the leadership of Jomo Kenyatta for immediate independence."

He resumed his political and trade union activities in November 1961. He joined the Kenya Freedom Party, an associate organisation of Kenya African National Union.

He resumed his membership of the Printing and Kindred Trade Workers' Union (of which he was one of the founders). He joined KANU when the doors of membership opened to all irrespective of race, colour or creed on October 21, 1962 (KFP voluntarily dissolved itself a few days later).

Makhan Singh was elected as Chairman of the Legislative Committee of Kenya Federation of Labour (KFL) and was a KFL representative on the committee which drafted Kenya's Industrial Relations in 1962.

After his release he actively worked for the unity of the national movement through KANU and for unity of the trade union movement through KFL and for their mutual unity, co-operation and solidarity with the National Government under the premiership of Jomo Kenyatta.

When Kenya was declared as an independent nation on December 12,1963, he felt happy that the second goal in his life had been attained. Through KANU and KFL he wanted to build a strong united, democratic African socialist Kenya, East Africa and ultimately the whole of Africa.

Advice to the South Asian Community

On his return from India, Makhan Singh had the insight to see that the South Asian community ensconced between the White settlers and the Black majority would be caught in political tensions. He wrote an article to set out tasks that they could address for the decade ahead.

They should work with the Africans for democratic advancement, which would establish a democratic government with equal franchise and adult suffrage.

They should organise joint fronts of Indian associations, African political unions, Pakistani organisations, trade unions of all workers and youth leagues.

They should work towards establishment of common high schools where all children should learn Kiswahili. Children should be taught the best of South Asian culture and African culture.

Much of these could not happen because Kenya's State of Emergency in the 1950s. In the 1960s after independence, school segregation was ended in phases. But for Makhan Singh, there was more to this – he saw this as a salvation for the South Asian Community.

Kenya's Trajectory of Development

British colonisation of Kenya was a conquest by force of arms which overcame all the resistance from the communities from the coast to the hinterland through the encroachment on ancestral lands.

Conquest meant rapid transformation in the system of production, of trade, of the economy. The building of the railway opened up Kenya to the world market and also opened up the internal market.

The land grab of the most fertile tracts up in the highlands led to the growth of plantations of coffee, tea, and other crops aimed largely at the British home market.

The opening up of the rural areas enabled the penetration of merchant capital largely owned by South Asians to accumulate through trade with the peasantry by buying local produce in exchange for essential commodities such as blankets, clothes, household goods, and building materials. There was enormous growth of the cash economy.

The growth of villages into towns, and some towns into larger cities, and the attendant urbanisation with its construction of buildings for commercial purposes and for accommodation by itself led to capital accumulation. These centres of population were connected by railways and roads. With the coming of cars and trucks, rapid transportation accelerated commerce.

The historical material basis of the life of Kenyans, their consumption of food, their habitation, their social reproduction was transformed within a generation or two. Societal relations became complex as a result of the change in the system of production, of commerce, of agriculture and industry.

The British authorities embedded capitalist relations in all aspects of life. Private property in land and business was central to this. With this came banks, credit and finance to accelerate development. Monopoly capital dominated the world and penetrated Kenya. Major corporations were open for business in Kenya in all sectors.

The colonial state was highly centralised with the Governor-General exercising ultimate executive power. The civil service and departmental ministries administered the country at local and national level. The power to raise taxation and defray state expenditure lay with the executive.

The criminal justice system based on British law ensured law and order. The courts and prisons were well embedded. The police, army and the air force safeguarded national security. The intelligence services kept the country under surveillance.

The transfer of power to the Kenyatta government after the 1961 elections was seamless, without any dramatic change. There was the new national flag, a new sense of patriotism among the masses, new ministers, new officials but the state machinery, the system of production, the key ministries remained as they were. The transformation of Kenya was conservative, nor revolutionary.

Independent Kenya was born as a dependency of the British and continues to remain so. The policy makers were trained by the British and later by the United States, largely following similar monetary and fiscal policies.

The new ruling class took up its role of governing this inheritance. There were opportunities for them in every field. They could buy land, property, own shares in business. So we had the growth of the black elite at the same time as the increase in inequality and poverty on the other end.

The oil crisis of 1970s followed by the neo-liberal turn by Ronald Reagan and Margaret Thatcher administrations in the US and UK, respectively, gave finance capital a free hand to push for globalisation across the world. Many global south countries faced a debt driven crisis. The International Monetary Fund and World Bank quickly followed suit, imposing austerity regimes through structural adjustment programmes. Out went free schooling, health care, agriculture subsidies, etc.

The microelectronics revolution ushered in a new global mode of production with capital even more centralised. Capital could move freely across national boundaries to exploit labour across the world to maximise the surplus it could accumulate. It can choose the cheapest labour pool to put it to work. Globalisation accelerated and further increased poverty across the board.

During the Daniel arap Moi years, Kenya's economic growth collapsed from 7.6 per cent in 1979 to 5.6 per cent in 1980. Kenya's growth did not pick up thereafter under his reign. To manage the crisis, he became increasingly dictatorial and was not averse to detaining and torturing opponents. The state machine was always primed for this since independence.

Growth declined much further in the 1990s. By early 2002, when Moi was leaving office, growth had dropped to 0.6 per cent.

Kenya's population has rocketed from about 8 million in 1962 to 55 million in 2023. The fruits of economic growth have been captured by 0.1 per cent of the population where 8,300 persons own more wealth than the bottom 99.9 per cent. The richest 10 per cent of people in Kenya earn an average 23 times more than the poorest 10 per cent.

Kenya's alignment with US and UK imperialism allows foreign bases and training on its soil. With the decades-long instability in Somalia, Kenya has sent its troops into its northern neighbour to fight the Al-Shabab group. It has also sent a brigade to the Democratic Republic of Congo and police to Haiti to stabilise the country.

In the long term, this is untenable. With looming existential threats to Kenyan society such as climate change and phasing out fossil fuels, the government will need to fashion policies for the public good rather than private profit.

The Marginalisation of the Left in Kenyan Politics

With its emergence as the sole superpower after the Second World War, the US set itself three objectives: its primacy over the other leading capitalist countries in Europe, Japan and others; the containment/ disappearance of communist states; and the defeat of economic nationalism in the Third World. It has been remarkably successful.

It set out to defeat the Left across the world -- whether communist or nationalist. Any independent Left movement was seen as a threat. Kenya was no exception. Kenyatta continued to treat Makhan Singh as a dangerous revolutionary and marginalized him. It is ironic that Makhan Singh, who was the first to call for independence in 1950, "uhuru sasa", and was locked away for 11.5 years as punishment, has been treated in this way.

Radical leaders such as Kimaathi, Makhan Singh, Bildad Kaggia, Fred Kubai, Pio Gama Pinto, as well as progressive organisations such as Mau Mau and the radical trade unions, with a vision for a just and equal society that they aspired to were forcibly removed from the scene by a triumphant government allied to imperialism.

Regretfully, Pio Gama Pinto, one of the most prominent left politicians active in the Kenyan Parliament was assassinated in 1965. In 1966, the left wing faction of KANU broke off to form the Kenya People's

Union, a socialist party under the leadership of Oginga Odinga. The party had wide support in the country with most districts having a KPU MP. Kenyatta manoeuvred to ban KPU in 1969 with its leader arrested and all branches dissolved.

What We Can Learn from Makhan Singh's Life and Work

In spite of all the efforts of the colonial government both in India and Kenya, and the independent government in Kenya to silence Makhan Singh and marginalise him, comrades have reclaimed his life and work over the past two decades. He was an avid researcher of history, leaving behind seminal work on the history of trade unions in East Africa. His leaflets, articles, poetry provide us with insight into his thinking and actions. His recent biography by Zarina Patel (2006) and consistent research and publications by Shiraz Durrani provide us with the many-sided perspectives on an exceptional revolutionary.

In his short working life of 37 years, Makhan Singh was imprisoned or detained for 16 years (nearly 40 per cent) leaving him 21 years of freedom in society. The last 10 years of his life were in semi-retirement. Just imagine the time taken from him that he could have used to achieve much more.

The central feature of his life and work was his immense dedication to the working class. He had an unshakeable belief that they were the producers of wealth in any given society and should have the power to determine their conditions of work, remuneration and redistribution of the wealth among other working people. This required moving beyond a capitalist society where capitalists privately control production of goods and services. They pay workers a wage after extracting a surplus, which provides them with expenses and profits. He shared this conviction with the founders of modern socialism — Karl Marx and Frederick Engels.

Makhan Singh believed that the working class should be highly organised using all the best means of communication such as newsletters, handbills, etc in its campaigning. It had to resist any intimidation from employers. Its strength lay in collective action. It should fight against any injustices and better living wages united as a class fully understanding what the capitalist class do. The point was always to change things under given circumstances.

The racial hierarchy of the colonial British Empire was anathema to him. He found this an instrument to divide and rule workers. He believed that workers united across racial boundaries fighting together could change the system. When he became the General Secretary of the Indian Trade Union in May 1935, he transformed it into the Labour Trade Union of Kenya (LTUK) open to all workers irrespective of race, religion and colour. This was a landmark moment for the unity of the working class. By 1937, the union had expanded its reach to all over East Africa to become Labour Trade Union of East Africa (LTUEA). Its membership expanded rapidly.

In all his work he showed what an exceptional and single-minded campaigner he was. Presciently, LTUK launched the campaign to limit the working day to eight hours after a lot of publicity in the community and unions in October 1936. After 10 days of campaigning, most employers acceded to the demand.

Makhan was convinced that in the struggle between the capitalist class and working class, the capitalist always suppresses wages while the working class is always contending to maintain its living standards against price increases in basic necessities.

The success of the LTUK strike in 1937 was a great achievement under the leadership of Makhan Singh. Makhan Singh was deeply convinced that the trade union movement should not restrict itself to workplace wage, and working conditions demands. Their demands ought to stretch to the provision of education, housing, health, etc. These demands can only be met if the working class can win political power. Linking the economic and political struggle was vital for the national liberation of Kenya. Capitalism always sought to keep these two separate – and continues to work at it even today. Working class unity was vital here. The East African Trade Union Congress founding in May 1949 became a nerve centre of militant activists until 1952 when all unions were proscribed. He was always politically active in different parties to influence their work.

Connecting workers across different nations was another strand of his work. He made international connections with the British Trade Union Congress, the South African Trades and Labour Council and the International Labour Office. Besides these, he had innumerable connections with the political and trade union movement in India.
On his return to India in 1940, he threw himself energetically into the

Indian freedom struggle showing that he saw the struggle for freedom in Kenya and India as being intrinsically connected. He was active underground and was arrested in May 1940 and detained for four and a half years.

This demonstrated that Makhan Singh was a fearless and courageous person. On his return to Kenya, surviving two attempts by the colonial authorities to deport him, he made the first ever public call for the full independence of Kenya at a conference on April 23. This was enough for the authorities to impose restrictions on his freedom for more than 11 and a half years.

Throughout his life, Makhan Singh was an uncompromising votary of non-violence. In his fight against the contemptible colonial government, he never advocated the use of violence. It was often the colonial authorities who provoked violence by gunning down peaceful unarmed protestors.

Above all, throughout his life he shunned self-enrichment. He was incorruptible. He spent an enormous amount of time organising the trade union movement in Kenya without any payment. When he was in detention in Kenya, he was visited by prison officers, district commissioners and other colonial agents making him offers either to leave Kenya or recant and start working against the Kenyan workers' movement to be rewarded. He refused such offers. After independence, he supported the Kenyatta government without asking for any favours in return.

He wrote of Nairobi, a city where he grew up, lived and worked when it was granted city status in 1954:

> There are two Nairobi's – that of the rich and that of the poor. The status of the latter has not changed... celebrations [to make status of City for Nairobi] will be justified on the day when the country's Government become truly democratic, with the workers fully sharing the tasks of government.

He saw the social inequality in Nairobi, the segregation in housing, the distribution of wealth as unjust.

What Kind of Society Do We Want in Kenya?

We can see in the reflection on the life of Makhan Singh and his critical thoughts that Kenya, shrouded in capitalism for four generations, does not do justice to its people. Kenya has failed to provide an environment in which all its people can flourish, enjoy security and life.

Power is highly centralised in Kenya. Its wealth is controlled by a small elite. The fruits of growth end up in the pockets of the wealthy and the corporations that dominate the economy. Those workers who produce the wealth of the country receive the least for their labour. Their lives are insecure. They do not enjoy the best of an education service, the health service, or housing in the city.

Democracy is a sham. It is managed and controlled by the rich. The media manipulate public opinion to manufacture consent in politics. Public debate is limited within narrow confines. Local government has been failing for years. It is often forgotten that capitalism has made private property a world power. All production is in the private hands of corporations. All built structures, factories, offices and homes are privately owned. Private property has been made sacrosanct and legally protected even when many lands in such areas as the White Highlands were looted from indigenous people.

Only socialist policies can provide for the needs of all Kenyans. Yet internationally, the balance of forces has shifted dramatically. The fall of the Soviet Union in 1991 marked the great defeat of socialism. The turn of China to capitalist development marked the triumph of neo-liberal capitalism. Many governments which were dependent on the Soviet Union collapsed. Most communist parties dissolved or are severely weakened.

United States returned on the world stage as the sole superpower and used the opportunity to launch wars against Afghanistan, Iraq, Libya, Syria to assert its hegemony and capture fossil fuel resources. The long war in Yemen in alliance with the Kingdom of Saudi Arabia continues with terrible consequences. With widespread use of financial sanctions against many countries, the US has used financial strangulation to quash any socialist development, e.g. in Venezuela. The Ukraine-Russia war over the expansion of NATO has already affected food production across the world, leading to greater food insecurity in the Global South because of a rise in fertiliser prices.

But the world is in flux, with the situation ever changing. The world is full of explosive contradictions. Two existential threats -- climate change and possible nuclear war -- loom large.

Left forces in Kenya should never give up hope. This is the time for organising. The efforts made to research, archive history with the aim to educate the masses are progressive. The opening of justice centres and libraries giving people access to books and publications from the Left perspective is vital.

Kenyan society is full of contradictions — between rich and poor; between capitalists and workers; between workers and peasants; between land owners and the landless; between the state and people; between representative democracy and grass roots democracy; between the homeless and homeowner, etc. Each contradiction needs to be analysed in its particularity and how it can be resolved.

Organising people around such contradictions is the beginning. Community groups campaigning for clean water, better housing, educational opportunities, and better health provision need to be built. Such initiatives require organising by cadres with the calibre of Makhan Singh. And such organising needs to be systematic and long term, building the confidence of people. It is through these kinds of communities of resistance that the state should be challenged, its weaknesses exposed.

If one encounters failure, then one should learn from it to come back with better strategies. As the communities of resistance grow, modern means of communication should be deployed. Wide ranging literature should be published setting out the path towards socialism in Kenya. Organic intellectuals should be cultivated and given voice. Mechanisms should be set up to challenge the mass media and hold it to account.

The development of grassroots democracy should be a central theme to counter the highly centralised state. There are so many exciting possibilities here. For example, developments among the Kurdish people of 'democratic confederalism' where a community exercises self determination through direct democracy with participation of women (feminist) and all ethnic minorities (multiculturalism) equally with a cooperative economy and the greatest care of ecology is getting a lot of attention across the world.

This would lay the basis for a nationwide Left party. A party that would give hope that it can bring about changes for all the people in Kenya to create a more just and equal society. Without preparation to take power, without engaging in struggle, we cannot win power.

The capitalist ruling class will ever be vigilant and do everything in its power to destroy any progressive movement. It has the money and the apparatus of surveillance such as intelligence services to do this. It would work closely with US and UK intelligence services to ensure that nothing emerges to challenge the status quo. Revolutionaries should know their enemies and be equally vigilant. They should develop their own network for obtaining intelligence of what is going on in the society at large. They should safeguard their own structure against penetration by secret agents. They should understand how counter-revolution has worked across the world to destroy progressive revolutions.

References

Anderson, David (2005): *Histories of the Hanged: The Dirty War in Kenya and the End of Empire*. London: Weidenfield & Nicolson.

Durrani, Shiraz (2006): *Never be Silent: Publishing & Imperialism in Kenya, 1884-1963.* London: Vita Books.

Durrani, Shiraz (2015, Ed.) *Makhan Singh: A Revolutionary Trade Unionist.* London: Vita Books. 2015.

Elkins, Caroline (2005): *Britain's Gulag: The brutal end of Empire in Kenya*. London: Random House.

Kinyatti, Maina wa (2019): *History of Resistance in Kenya, 1884-2002.* Nairobi: Mau Mau Research Centre.

Paice Edward (2008): *Tip and Run: The Untold Tragedy of the First World War in Africa* London: Weidenfeld & Nicolson.

Marx in Punjabi Translation

Amarjit Chandan[53]

In the early twentieth century, the Punjabis studying at the universities of Oxford, Cambridge, London and California established contact and interaction with Western thought. The poet Puran Singh (1881--1931) engaged Nietzsche in Punjabi; the great lexicographer Kahan Singh (1861--1938) collaborated with Macauliffe (1837--1913) on the English translation of the Sikh scriptures for his six-volume magnum opus *The Sikh Religion*; the Greek and Sanskrit scholar Dharam Anant [Singh] worked on Plato; and Santokh Singh (1892--1927) introduced Marx into the world of Punjabi letters.

Bhai Santokh Singh (the honorific title commonly used for Ghadar activists) was one of the founders of the communist movement in the Punjab. He served as the general secretary of the Ghadar Party from March 1914 to August 1922. In April 1918, he was tried with 29 other Ghadarites in the Indo-German or San Francisco Hindu Conspiracy Case and was sentenced to 21 months' rigorous imprisonment. In the McNeil's Island prison, he came into contact with other political inmates – Russian communist exiles and activists of the Industrial Workers of the World. He spent his time in the prison reading several leftist books, including the three volumes of *Capital.*[54] After his release, he travelled to the Soviet Union, where he enrolled in the KUTV – University of the Toilers of the East. After returning to Punjab, he started *Kirti* (The Worker) in 1926, a Punjabi magazine that was published in the Gurmukhi script.

Santokh Singh was the first Punjabi writer and journalist who coined and used new words with roots in Sanskrit in his articles published in *Kirti*. In its first issue, dated February 1926, he published a short introductory article on Dialectical and Historical Materialism. The essay was also an important milestone in the development of Punjabi literary and political prose. Prior to this, historical and political discourse in the Punjabi letters had mainly appeared in the form of poetry.

53 Amarjit Chandan (b. 1946, Nairobi) is a writer, poet, translator, journalist and activist who has lived in London since 1980.

54 Josh, Sohan Singh, *Ghadar party da Ithas* [History] Vol 1 as quoted in Ghadri Yodha [Ghadri Fighter] Bhai Santokh Singh: Jivan ate Likhtan [Life & Letters], Jalandhar: Desh Bhagat Yadgar Committee, 2003.

Bhagat Singh Studied Marx

Dwarka Das Library, which shifted from Lahore to Delhi to Chandigarh after Partition, has in its collection the first English edition of *Capital*. It is a fair conjecture that Bhagat Singh would have accessed it. In his memoir, *Yash ki Dharohar* (Heritage of Honour, 1988), Bhagwan Das Mahaur, an accomplice of Bhagat Singh, writes that he had read *Capital* on the suggestion of Bhagat Singh, but could not comprehend it at all. Bhagat Singh's *Jail Notebooks* include quotes from the writings of Marx and Engels. Probably he had borrowed these from Upton Sinclair's 700-page long *Cry for Justice*, which he had read thoroughly in the prison.[55]

First Punjabi Translation

Makhan Singh (1913--1973) a whole-timer of the CPI during 1939-1947, contributed significantly to the theoretical work of the party. He spent his time in translating Marx's *Das Kapital* into Punjabi in the Gurmukhi script. In 1942, Jagjit Singh Anand, an editor of *Jang-e-Azadi,* the CPI organ, received Makhan Singh's Punjabi translation of 'Dialectical Materialism', a chapter in *Das Kapital*. In his memoir, Anand recalled his deep impression of Makhan Singh's nuanced grasp of Marxist theory as well as his mastery of the Punjabi language. The two men worked on the editorial board of *Jang-e-Azadi* until 1947, when Makhan Singh left Punjab for Kenya.[56]

No more information is available except this brief mention of the Punjabi translation of *Capital* done in the early 1940s. The manuscript was never published. There is no trace of any workbook of the translation in the archives of Makhan Singh, meticulously maintained by his family.

***

55 Lal, Chaman (2019) Ed., *The Bhagat Singh Reader*, Noida, HarperCollins.

56 Interview with Piyo Rattansi, 2003, as quoted in *Unquiet: The Life & Times of Makhan Singh,* Zarina Patel (ed), Nairobi: Zand, 2006.

ਸਾਥੀ ਕਾਰਲ ਮਾਰਕਸ
ਪੁਰਾਣੀ
ਤੇ
ਨਵੀਂ ਦੁਨੀਆਂ
ਪਬਲਿਸ਼ਰਜ਼:-ਸਰਜੀਤ ਐਂਡ ਕੰਪਨੀ
ਰੇਲਵੇ ਰੋਡ, ਜਾਲੰਧਰ ਸ਼ਹਿਰ ।
ਦਾਦ ੧੦੦੦
ਮੁੱਲ-ਚਾਰ ਆਨੇ

Old & the New World by 'Comrade' Karl Marx in Punjabi, 1937. Dyal Singh Memorial Library Lahore Collection

The editorial board of *Jang-e-Azadi* consisted of communist activists and pioneer Punjabi translators of Marxian literature, including Bhag Singh, a PhD in political science from Berkeley University, Teja Singh Sutantar, a legendary political leader and graduate of the University of the Toilers of the East Moscow, Makhan Singh, Jagjit Singh Anand, and Randhir Singh.

In May 1937 a collection of articles on capitalism, imperialism and socialism published in *Kirti* was compiled by Harkishan Singh Surjeet. This 100-page book was titled ਪੁਰਾਣੀ ਤੇ ਨਵੀ ਦੁਨੀਆਂ (*Old & the New World*) and its author's name was given as Sathi (Comrade) Karl Marx. It was the first Marxian text in Punjabi that was laden with the new terminology of economics and philosophy, not familiar to most Punjabi readers at the time. Most of the newly-coined terms stuck. But a hundred years later, there is still no consensus about certain words and concepts. For instance, the word "Capital" can be translated both as "Poonji" (org. Sanskrit) and "Sarmaya" (org. Farsi).

***

The first authentic Punjabi translation of *Capital* was published in 1975 by Navyug publishers, Delhi. The three volumes were translated by a team of fulltime employees of the Soviet Embassy's Information section. Vol 1 was translated by Piara Singh Sehrai, Prem Singh, Karanjit Singh and Gurbachan Singh Bhullar; Vol 2 was translated solely by Karanjit Singh and Vol 3 was translated by Gurbachan Singh Bhullar. The problem of translating foreign words and concepts into Punjabi posed a significant problem to the translators, who frequently struggled to arrive at a consensus. In all three volumes, Avtar Singh Malhotra, general secretary of the Punjab unit of CPI, was outlined as the vetter of the translation process. But this was likely just a formality. Needless to say, the whole project was directly sponsored by Soviet Russians.[57]

57 Gurbachan Singh Bhullar phone chat with the author on September 10 2022. Later, on his own initiative, he published *A Dictionary of Economics and Politics* in Punjabi in 1985.

Cover of *Capital* in Punjabi translation Sarmaya, 1975. Reprinted 2013

No other book by Marx except *The Poverty of Philosophy* was published in Punjabi translation.

The Communist Manifesto by Marx and Engels was first translated into Punjabi in the Gurmukhi script by Randhir Singh and published in Lahore in 1946.

***

Two Languages, Two Scripts

No Marxian text has been translated into Punjabi in the Farsi script in West Punjab Pakistan. A colloquial booklet of basic information about Marxism, titled *Nirvar*, was published by Rashid Uz Zaman in the Farsi script in Lahore (circa 1970). Unlike the East Punjabi translation, which largely relies on Sanskrit, Zaman's translation of Marxian terms borrowed heavily from Arabic and Farsi. This has long been a serious bone of contention between academics, linguists and writers on both sides of the international border.

•

[September 12, 2022]

The 1950 General Strike in Kenya-- Enter the Era of Militancy

Nicholas Mwangi

What a time to reflect on Makhan Singh! As I pen this reflection, revisiting the 1950 general strike, several significant international events are unfolding. The United Auto Workers (UAW) union has initiated a strike targeting Ford, General Motors, and Stellantis in the United States. This strike aims to exert pressure on these carmakers to concede higher wages and implement other improvements in their new labour agreements. Meanwhile, in Hollywood, writers are on strike, demanding increased royalties for their work, commonly referred to as residuals, and seeking stronger safeguards against the encroachment of artificial intelligence. In Kenya, Central Organisation of Trade Unions (COTU-K) has just issued a statement condemning a headline article critiquing the organisation, titled 'Death of Trade Unions: Why Workers Are Losing Their Influence'. They deem it misleading.

As we reflect on the momentous events of the 1950 General Strike in Kenya, it is important to recognise its profound significance in the context of the struggle for workers' rights and national independence. The General Strike in Kenya's history was not just a labour strike but a symbolic statement against the injustices of British colonial rule. To fully appreciate its impact, we must first understand the role of trade unions and their visionary leaders, such as Makhan Singh, played in shaping the course of Kenyan history. It is also important to understand the historical context of the time when the 1950 general strike took place. It was under British colonial rule, characterised by systemic economic exploitation, racial discrimination, and political oppression that severely marginalised the African population.

Trade unions have always played a crucial role in advocating workers' rights and shaping the socio-political landscape of many nations. In Kenya, trade unions like the Labour Trade Union of Kenya, the African Workers Federation, and the East African Trade Union Congress were instrumental in mobilising workers and championing their cause. In addition, as noted by (Ong'wen 2022, p.176), leaders such as Makhan Singh, Fred Kubai, Shah Mohammed, and Chege Kibacia were not only labour leaders; they were also ardent nationalists who understood the connection between labour rights and the broader struggle for independence. Further, (Durrani, 2018, p.31) asserts that the greatest weapon that the working class brought to the colonial battlefield --- potentially more powerful than the colonial armoured cars and planes -- was the actual and threatened withdrawal of their labour on which capitalist exploitation was based.

The Mau Mau armed struggle, another defining event in Kenya's struggle for independence, was also significantly influenced by the trade unions. Trade unions provided not only an ideological backbone but also a structural and organisational foundation for the broader anti-colonial struggle. Trade union leaders and activists recognised that British colonial rule systematically oppressed the Kenyan working class and dispossessed the majority of Africans of their land and rights. By mobilising workers around shared grievances such as poor wages, land alienation, and systemic racial discrimination, trade unions cultivated a strong sense of solidarity and resistance that permeated the Mau Mau movement.

The stage for the strike had been set by previous labour actions, including the 1939 Mombasa strike and the 1947, 12-day General Strike, led by the African Workers Federation. These strikes highlighted issues such as poor housing, low pay, racial discrimination, and police harassment, among others, affecting over 15,000 workers (Ong'wen 2022, p.176). Thus, the 1950 General Strike was not an isolated event but rather a culmination of years of action against grievances, economic exploitation, and political oppression. At its core, the strike was a protest against the injustices of the colonial system, including unfair labour practices and racial discrimination. Kenyan workers employed various tactics, including strikes, boycotts, picketing, and even sabotage, to force political crises and to advance the nationalist anti-colonial struggle.

The trigger for the strike was the banning of the East African Trade Union Congress (EATUC) on May 15, 1950, which marked a turning point. The arrest and imprisonment of EATUC's General Secretary, Makhan Singh, and its President, Fred Kubai set off the strike. Makhan Singh was regarded as the intellectual force behind the trade union movement. In response, the workers organised a nationwide strike, demanding the immediate release of their leaders, a new minimum wage, the abolition of repressive taxicab by-laws, an end to arbitrary arrests, and unconditional national independence for Kenya, Uganda, and Tanganyika. The strike, involving over 100,000 workers, greatly tested the colonial economy (Ong'wen 2022, p.178).

The General Strike of 1950, as documented by Makhan Singh in his 1969 book, *History of Trade Union Movement to 1952*, bore witness to an extraordinary display of solidarity and empathy among the Kenyan people. The striking workers and their families were not left to fend for themselves; instead, they received generous support from fellow citizens who provided food and other essentials in solidarity. Furthermore, on May 17, 1950, a symbolic act ignited the flame of resistance in Pumwani and Shauri Moyo, Nairobi. A bonfire was lit, symbolising the indomitable spirit of the strikers and, by extension, the collective determination of the Kenyan people to secure their freedom and independence. In the days that followed, the strike intensified, with subsequent actions on the May 18 and 19. Another key moment was marked on May 20, 1950, when approximately 750 African railway employees refused to report for duty and joined the strike. It became abundantly clear that all sections of the workforce were now actively participating in the strike, transcending boundaries and affiliations. The momentum of the movement was unstoppable.

In response to the growing unrest, the colonial government, perhaps sensing the magnitude of the situation, attempted to end the strike by proposing an increase in the minimum wage. However, the strike committee and trade union leaders, who had witnessed the power of collective action, deemed this offer, in the context of the other demands, insufficient. They recognised that while the strike had made a powerful statement, the struggle for justice and independence was far from over. Despite numerous arrests of strikers, the resolve of the workers remained unshaken. They understood that their demands were not merely economic but deeply rooted in their aspiration for a liberated and sovereign Kenya. The strike endured, withstanding attempts at suppression, and carried on with unwavering determination.

Ultimately, the General Strike of 1950 concluded on Thursday, May 25, marking an end to a monumental chapter in Kenya's history. This extraordinary display of unity and resolve had resonated nationwide, becoming one of the most significant events for the working class and peasants in Kenya. The strike was not just a protest; it was a statement of intent, a declaration that the people of Kenya were willing to endure great hardships to secure their rights and, ultimately, their freedom. Two years later, on October 20, 1952, the British colonial government declared a State of Emergency in Kenya in response to the emergence of the revolutionary movement -- Mau Mau -- that waged armed struggle in the fight for independence. The 1950 strike was one of the early signs of unrest and resistance against British colonial rule in Kenya. This strike, along with other acts of civil disobedience, marked the beginning of a more organised and militant phase of the struggle for independence.

In retrospect, while the trial of Makhan Singh, Fred Kubai and Chege Kibacia continued, resulting in their unjust detention, the 1950 General Strike in Kenya remains a turning point in the nation's history. It was a potent symbol of the synergy between the trade union movement and the struggle for national independence. The dedication of leaders like Makhan Singh and the resilience of Kenyan workers in the face of adversity laid the foundation for future political and social change. This strike serves as a reminder of the power of collective action, the importance of workers' rights, and the indomitable spirit of those who dare to challenge injustice and domination that can be emulated by the working class today.

References

Durrani, Shiraz (2018). *Trade Unions in Kenya's War of Independence*. Nairobi, Kenya Vita Books.

Makhan Singh (1969). *History of Kenya's Trade Union Movement to 1952*. Nairobi: East African Publishing House.

Ong'wen, Oduor (2022). *Stronger Than Faith.* Nairobi: Vita Books.

Remembering A Champion of Workers' Rights

Wacira Gatheru[60]

MADRASCOURIER.COM
Makhan Singh: The Sikh Revolutionary Who Fought For Kenya's Liberation | Madras Courier

Makhan Singh, a prominent labour leader and political activist, left an indelible mark on the labour movement in Kenya during the colonial

60 Wacira Gatheru is a highly accomplished writer, director, editor, and creative consultant with a strong background in the fashion and advertising industries. With a passion for creative problem-solving, Wacira brings a unique vision and skill set to every project. As a writer, Wacira has been recognised for his exceptional talent, receiving awards for his short films. Notably, his work on *The Strange Visitor* earned a nomination for Best Special Effects at the 9th Kalasha Awards. Additionally, his film *Mwikali* secured Second Place at the esteemed Machakos Film Festival. Wacira's editing expertise has been instrumental in various projects, including Dreamchild, KERU, FIHI, and Discovery +254, as well as numerous TV shows and feature-length movies across Kenya and East Africa. His meticulous attention to detail and artistic sensibility shine through in his work. Wacira's most recent creation, the short film, *The Girl Inside*, has gained international recognition and is currently being showcased at film festivals worldwide. Its selection for this year's First-Time Filmmaker Sessions @Pinewood Studios is a testament to Wacira's talent and dedication to his craft. Wacira has collaborated with renowned production houses, including Sounds & Pictures, Film Crew In Africa, Zamaradi, and more. His distinct creative flair has also led him to direct captivating music videos, earning high praise and significant viewership on platforms like YouTube, particularly for Veryl Mkali Wao. His passion, innovation, and commitment to excellence make him an invaluable asset to any project he undertakes. (Links To My Channels: Music Cinema Entertainment https://www.youtube.com/@m.c.e Zile Tales https://www.youtube.com/channel/UC_Vhko8ztENRTpNoziE7Log)

period. This paper explores the life and contributions of Makhan Singh in Kenya, his legacy in the country, the extent to which Kenyans remember him today, and strategies for raising awareness about his significant contributions to labour rights and social justice.

Makhan Singh was a charismatic and dedicated labour leader who played a pivotal role in advocating workers' rights in Kenya during the colonial era. His efforts in organising labour unions and leading strikes left a profound impact on the labour movement in the country. This paper seeks to shed light on his life, his role in Kenya, and the ways in which his legacy is remembered or forgotten in Kenya today. Makhan Singh arrived in Kenya during a time when Indian workers were subjected to harsh working conditions and low wages on British-owned farms and plantations.
Makhan Singh actively organised and led labour unions among Indian labourers in Kenya. His work in Kenya had a lasting influence on the labour movement in the country. His efforts laid the groundwork for more organised and powerful labour unions in post-independence Kenya.

While Makhan Singh's contributions to Kenya's labour movement are historically significant, his memory has faded to over the years. There are several reasons for this:

Shifting Focus: After gaining independence in 1963, Kenya's focus shifted to nation-building and addressing new challenges, and the history of the labour movement received comparatively less attention.

Limited Education: Many Kenyans, especially the younger generation, are not adequately educated about Makhan Singh and his contributions. He is not as prominently featured in the national curriculum as other historical figures.

In order to ensure that Makhan Singh's legacy is not forgotten and that Kenyans are aware of his significant contributions, the following strategies can be considered:

Inclusion in Education: Incorporating Makhan Singh's story and contributions into the national curriculum would help educate students about this important figure in their history.
Public Memorials: Erecting memorials, plaques, or statues in prominent public spaces in Kenya would serve as a visual reminder of Makhan Singh's contributions.

Documentary and Cultural Initiatives: Producing documentaries, organising exhibitions, and encouraging cultural events that highlight Makhan Singh's life and work can help raise awareness.

Community Engagement: Engaging local communities and labour unions to commemorate Makhan Singh through annual events or seminars can keep his memory alive.

Makhan Singh's contributions to the labour movement in Kenya were instrumental in shaping the country's history. While he may not be as widely remembered as other historical figures, there are practical steps that can be taken to ensure that his legacy is preserved and celebrated for future generations. Through education, memorials, and community engagement, Kenyans can rediscover and appreciate the legacy of this champion of workers' rights.

Remebering Hindpal Singh Jabbal

Hindpal S Jabbal MSc., FIET

Hindpal Singh Jabbal is the doyen of the power sector in Kenya, having worked in the sector for more than 50 years at senior levels.

Born in Nairobi in 1937 to Makhan Singh, the renowned trade unionist and freedom fighter in Kenya and the Satwant Kaur, Hindpal spent his early years in Gurjrawala and Lahore (now in Pakistan), retuning to Nairobi in 1948 to complete 'A' Levels from Jamhuri High School in 1954, while his father was still in detention from 1950 to 1961.

After graduation in Electrical Engineering from the University of Roorkee in 1958, he completed MSc from Manchester University, UK. He worked with Kenya Power from 1961 to 1987 in various capacities rising to the post of Chief Engineer Planning before taking early retirement in 1987.

Between 1987 and 1991, and then again from 1994 to 1995, he was appointed as the General Manager and CEO of an electric utility in West Indies under a Commonwealth Secretarial assignment.

In 1998, Hindpal was appointed Technical Adviser to the Ministry of Energy under a World Bank funding project to assist the ministry in restructuring the power sector, in least-cost planning and coordinating the implementation of various generation and transmission projects.

In recognition of his long and distinguished service to the power sector, Hindpal was appointed by President Mwai Kibaki as the first Chairman of the newly constituted Energy Regulatory Commission (ERC) in July 2007 for a period of four years. He was responsible for the technical and economic regulation of the entire Energy sector, comprising of power, petroleum and renewable energy. He remained actively involved in the promotion and development of renewable energy resources in the region.

Hindpal Jabbal has been married to Joginder for 63 years and are the proud parents of Arvinder Jabbal (UK) Manmit Jabbal (K) and Nita Nanda (USA).

NB

Hindpal Jabbal passed away on January 1, 2025. Vita Books expresses it's deepest condolences to the family.

Hindpal Singh Jabbal

The Doyen of Kenya's Power Sector

I have had a long and distinguished carrier in Kenya's power sector spanning over 50 years embracing generation, transmission, and distribution of electricity. I was also Chairman of the Energy Regulatory Commission (ERC) in 2007-11, responsible for the technical and economic regulation of the entire energy sector, including power, petroleum, and renewable energy.

Born in Nairobi in February 1937 to Makhan Singh, the great freedom fighter, I left for India with my parents just at the beginning of the Second World War in 1939, when I was just over two years old. In India, my father Makhan Singh was arrested in Ahmedabad for his political activities both in Kenya and India. He was imprisoned in Deoli Camp for about two years and was restricted in his village Gharjakh, Distt. Gujranwala (now Pakistan) for another three years. He was finally released towards the end of 1944. From Gharjakh, we all moved to Model Town, Lahore, at my mother's parental place, where my younger sister Inderjit was born in July 1945. My father continued with his political activities for the freedom struggle of India and was Sub-Editor of *Jang-e-Azadi*, a weekly newspaper in Punjab.

I did most of my primary schooling in my village Gharjakh and then in Lahore. Just two weeks before the Partition, on July 31, 1947, I left Lahore for Bombay together with my parents, younger sister Inderjit, and my maternal grandfather, S Tara Singh Mahal. My father left for Kenya on about August 10, and celebrated India's Independence Day on board the ship, arriving in Kenya on August 22, 1947. Together with my mother, my sister and brother Swarajpal, who was born in January 1948 in Bombay, we stayed behind with my maternal uncle Dr HS Mahal, a celebrated forensic scientist in Maharashtra. We returned to Nairobi in April 1948 to join my father and my grandparents. According to my age and academic proficiency I should have joined the primary school (now City Primary) in Standard III. However because of lack of space in the primary school I had to regrettably jump two classes and join Government Asian High School (now Jamhuri High) in Standard. V. At that time I was barely 11, and had very little knowledge of the English language. This was very tough on me.

My father was arrested in 1950 for his political activities and was detained in remote parts of Kenya for more than 11 years, finally being released in October 1961, barely two months before my wedding to Joginder in December 1961. While my father was in detention, my mother, my sister and brother, and I were taken care of by my grandfather S Sudh Singh, who came to Kenya in 1920 as a carpenter with the Railways, and eventually opened a small printing press in 1930, specializing in the Punjabi language.

I did all my schooling in Nairobi and cleared my 'A' Levels in December 1954. Since my grandfather could not afford to send me to England for a degree course in engineering, I decided to go to Roorkee University, (now an IIT), in 1955 on an Indian Government cultural scholarship. I graduated from Roorkee in September. 1958 with a BE degree in electrical engineering.

For lack of training facilities in Kenya at that time I went back to India for a one-year post-graduate training in Ahmedabad, near Sabarmati. On my return from Ahmedabad in early 1960, I sought for a job with East African Power & Lighting Co (now Kenya Power), but there was no vacancy at that time. I therefore asked my grandfather to take a break and visit India for a well-deserved holiday, while I will ran his printing press.

I ultimately joined Kenya Power on January 1, 1961 as a Junior Engineer in the Protection Department. Towards the end of 1966, I completed my MSc in Power Systems from Manchester University as a Commonwealth Scholar, while still maintaining my services with Kenya Power. In 1968 I was appointed protection engineer, then chief engineer planning in 1973, and finally Corporate Planning Manager in 1979, responsible for least-cost planning and execution of all major generation and transmission projects in Kenya, including the first 3x15MW geothermal plant at Olkaria in 1981/82.

In 1987, I took early retirement from Kenya Power aged 50, and immediately thereafter I was competitively selected, General Manager and CEO of a utility in the West Indies, Dominica Electricity Supply Company, under a Commonwealth Secretariat assignment. I was in Dominica on two separate periods, between 1987-91, and then again in 1994-95.

In 1998, I was appointed Technical Adviser to the Ministry of Energy, Kenya, under a World Bank assignment to assist the ministry in restructuring the power sector; implementing various power projects based on least-cost power plan; adjusting electricity tariff; and generally improving the accountability and efficiency of the entire power sector. My contract came to an end in 2004.

In July 2007, I was appointed Chairman of Energy Regulatory Commission (ERC) by President Mwai Kibaki, in recognition of my long and distinguished service to the power sector both in Kenya and abroad. ERC was established in 2007 as an independent authority, under an Act of Parliament, to undertake technical, economic and legal regulation of the entire energy sector, including power, petroleum and renewable energy. I successfully completed my four-year term in 2011. Since the expiry of my term with ERC in 2011, I have remained fairly active professionally. I have been invited as a keynote speaker or sessional chairman in several international conferences in Africa and Europe. I have also published several authoritative articles on Kenya's power sector in the local press. Currently I am also involved in the development of various renewable energy projects in Kenya, such as geothermal, wind, solar and biomass, mainly in an advisory capacity.

I am a Registered Engineer in Kenya (R.Eng), a Fellow of Institution of Engineering and Technology of UK (FIET), and a Fellow of Economic Development Institute of World Bank (FEDI). At one time I was a Board Member of Engineers Board of Kenya, and Local Representative of the IET.

My Family

Joginder and I got married in 1961, and she has been my life partner since through thick and thin, giving birth to three children, all born in Nairobi. They are all happily married, and well settled in life.

Arvinder, our eldest son, born in 1962, is a trained accountant by profession, now settled in London, running his own practice under the name Jabbal & Co. He is married to Svetlana, a Ukrainian lady, who works with him.

Our second son, Manmit Jabbal, born in 1965, is a trained architect, settled in Nairobi, and is one of the top interior designers in the country, running his own practice under the name Ikon Designs. He is married to Dr Preeti Jabbal, who works in a leading hospital in Nairobi.

Our daughter, Nita Nanda, born in 1970, is a trained interior designer, now settled and working in Dallas, USA. She is married to Harjeet Nanda, who is a director with Ericsson, a large Swedish company My younger sister Dr Inderjit Gill, born in Lahore in 1945, used to work as a senior research scientist in bio-chemistry. Now retired, she is settled with her family in Nottingham.

My younger brother Swarajpal, born in Bombay in 1948, used to run his own mechanical workshop in Nairobi. He has now settled with his family in Perth, Australia.

Message to the Punjabis Living Abroad.

The Punjabis living abroad (Hindus, Sikhs and Muslims) have contributed immensely in spreading the rich cultural heritage of Punjab in three things—hot masala curry, 'bhangra' dance and music, and now 'salwar-kameez'.

In countries like Kenya, to which I belong, Punjabis were the first ones to come as a group in the 1890s during the colonial period. The majority of the first generation Punjabis built the Railways as artisans, worked in the Police Force as constables, and managed the Civil Service as junior administrators and clerks. They also opened the interior and went to remote parts of Kenya as traders and 'Dukawallas'. See Sharad Rao's book called *Indian Dukawallas*, published recently.

As the country developed, the second and subsequent generations of Punjabis have played a major role in politics, sports, trade, commerce, industry, road transport, farming and horticulture.

They have also contributed immensely to all the major professions as teachers, professors, engineers, technologists, architects, accountants, managers, doctors and lawyers. In fact the only two Chief Justices of Kenya of Asian origin were both Punjabis, namely, Justice Chunilal Madan and Justice Abdul Majid Cockar.

My advice to the younger generation of Punjabis, both from India and Pakistan, who are permanently settled abroad anywhere in the world, is to become part and parcel of the country of adoption as true citizens, while maintaining your cultural heritage. However, please discard the narrow prejudices and parochial politics of your country of origin.

HSJ/8.4.2017

Mungu Comrade, A Play – 'The Red Prophet'

Atamjit Singh

MUNGU COMRADE

A play by Atamjit

– based on life of Makhan Singh, the great Kenyan Freedom Fighter and Trade Unionist –

Mungu Comrade

***The Red Prophet*, A Play by Atamjit Singh (Review)**[58]

58 Reproduction from a handout at the reading of the play. Atamjit Singh: Born in 1950 at Amritsar, Atamjit is the author of three dozen short and full-length plays that seek to create dialogue at multiple levels of discourse, ranging from dialogue with the self, the society, and beyond with the cultural forces that define both self and society. He juxtaposes the past and the present, the historical and the contemporary, the collective folk idiom and the contesting individual voice. Atamjit's plays, even in the absence of overt political commitment, display social consciousness in a meaningful manner. His sensibility is transdisciplinary in his experiments with new themes and techniques but his works are anchored in human values that seek equality, justice, emancipation of women, communal amity and peaceful coexistence. Known for dramatic solo recitals of his texts, he also performed the plays throughout India and abroad. Honoured with the National Awards by the Sahitya Akademi and the Sangeet Natak Akademi, he was also declared as a Living Legend by the National School of Drama during the Theatre Olympiad, 2018, at Delhi.

Preface to 'The Red Prophet'

Ngugi wa Thiong'o

July 30, 2021

Makhan Singh after his release addressing workers, Nairobi. 1961. Photographer unknown
Available at: https://www.thebeacon.in/2021/07/30/the-red-prophet-a-play-by-atamjit-singh/

As a child growing up in the Kenya of the 1950s, I remember adults in the village whispering about an Indian Prophet who said that Independence or Uhuru would certainly come to the African people. This assertion, coming at the height of the repression of the Kenyan people by the white settler colonial state, was almost too bold to comprehend. It came across as myth, but it had the suggestive power of something coming from God, passed onto the people of Kenya, through this Indian prophet. I have written about this mythic Makhan Singh in my memories of childhood, titled *Dreams in a Time of War*.

But it was not myth, it was real. Makhan Singh was the first person to call for Uhuru Sasa for Kenya and other East African territories, and fearlessly defended the call at his political trial. Though an adherent of non-violence, still his prophetic call must have given hope and encouragement to the young men who had begun to train for the armed struggle that would later become known as Mau Mau. Kenya Land and Freedom Army was actually the name of the armed resistance, but the British coined the more mystical sounding Mau Mau. By the time the actual armed struggle began in and around 1952, and a State of Emergency declared, Makhan Singh was already exiled in Lodwar, Northern Kenya, where Jomo Kenyatta and the entire leadership of the anti-colonial nationalist resistance would later join him. For many years, he remained this mythic figure in my mind. I never thought I would ever meet him in real life. But I did once, in Nairobi, at a conference of the Kenya Historical Association to which I had been invited to speak. It was nine years after Independence, the Uhuru Sasa he had prophesied and for which he had been imprisoned for more than 10 years. I had already published my novels, *Weep Not Child, The River Between*, and *A Grain of Wheat,* and he had published his *History of Kenya's Trade Union Movement to 1952*.

The prophet of my childhood, the legend of Kenyan struggle, was this humble, this unassuming presence, but for me, no less impressive for looking ordinary. He was after all the ordinary who did extraordinary things ever since he set foot in Kenya in 1927. He would later involve himself in the politics of the working class; he would become known as the father of trade unionism in Kenya.

His remarkable story is the subject of this play, *The Red Prophet*, by Atamjit. It is epic in scope and conception, and Brechtian in its unfolding. It covers Makhan Singh's entire life in Kenya, but then his life is the life of the country, his story is the history of Kenya, his aspirations, those of the struggling peoples in Kenya, Africa and the world. His extraordinary life in the struggle is best summed by one of the characters: In his blood I saw nothing but humanity, only humanity.

The play is a fitting tribute to Makhan Singh. It is even more fitting that Mount Kenya, after which the country is named, is actually a character in this epic. The play is also an important addition to the literature of resistance, a tribute to the power of working people of the world, irrespective of their race and religion.

Khalsa Lakhvir Singh: Makhan Singh Exhibition

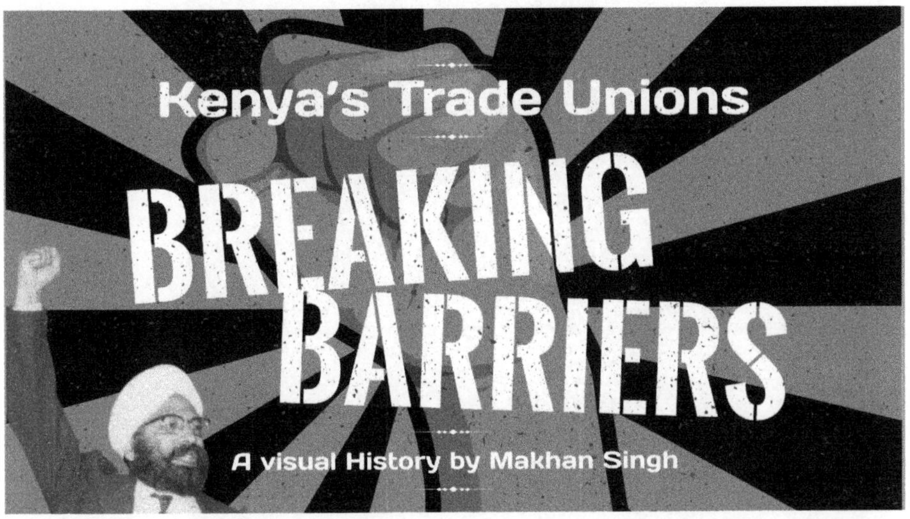

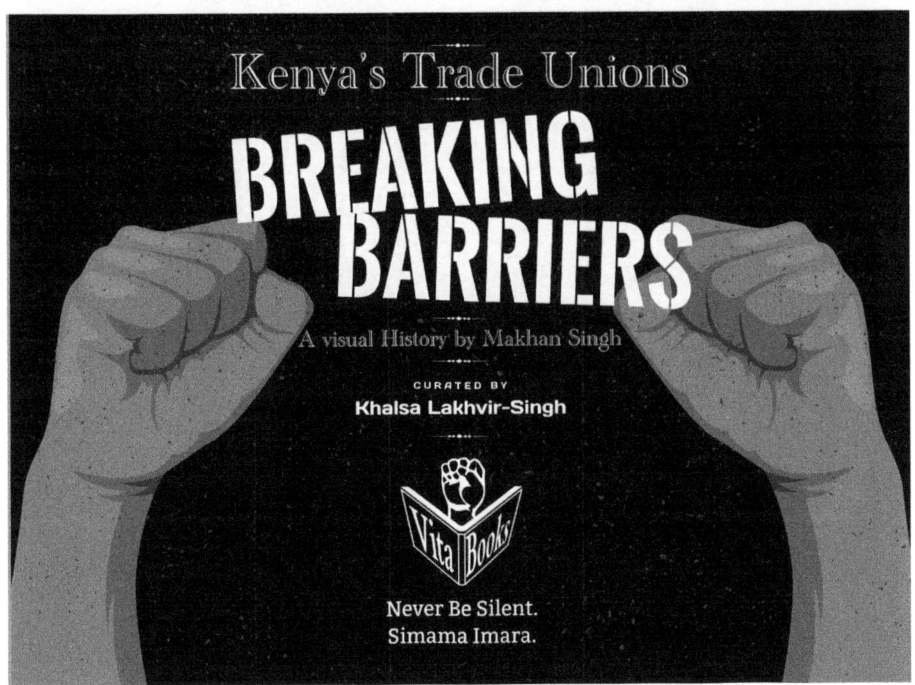

Contents

A visual History by Makhan Singh
LEGENDS OF THE REVOLUTION
I
AGGREY MINYA
ARTHUR OCHWADA
BILDAD KAGGIA
CHEGE KIBIRU
CHEGE KIBACHIA

A visual History by Makhan Singh
LEGENDS OF THE REVOLUTION
2
CLEMENT LUBEMBE
DISHON KAHIATO
ELIAS MAKANDU
FRED KUBAI
GEORGE K NDEGWA

A visual History by Makhan Singh
LEGENDS OF THE REVOLUTION
3
GERALD OGOLA
GICHURE GATAMA
GOPAL SINGH
GOVIND OKEDA
HARRY THUKU

A visual History by Makhan Singh
LEGENDS OF THE REVOLUTION
4
JAMES BEAUTTAH
JAMES KAREBE
JD KALI
JESSE KARIUKI
JOHN MUNGAI

A visual History by Makhan Singh
LEGENDS OF THE REVOLUTION
5
JOSEPH KANGETHE
JW OKAKAH
LIVINGSTONE KURIA
MAKHAN SINGH
MAO NDISI

A visual History by Makhan Singh
LEGENDS OF THE REVOLUTION
6
MELIKISADEK ANYANJE
MJ DEMAN
MWANGI MACHARIA
S OSORE
MUINDI MBINGU

LEGENDS OF THE REVOLUTION
7
SAMUEL MUHANJI
SHAH MOHAMED
TOM MBOYA
UJAGAR SINGH
WILLIE GEORGE

MOMENTS OF DEFIANCE
1
CONFERENCES
Third annual conference of the Labour Trade Union of East Africa held on the 23rd July 1939 on the open ground behind the Desai Memorial Hall, Nairobi.
BREAKING

MOMENTS OF DEFIANCE
4
JARDIN LTD.
25% INCREASE
STRIKES
A part of the workers' procession in Nairobi which took place on the 25th May 1937 during the strike.
BREAKING
BARRIERS

MOMENTS OF DEFIANCE
6
DEMONSTRATIONS
Workers' demonstration at the Nairobi Police Lines on 16th March 1922 to demand the release of **Harry Thuku**.
BREAKING BARRIERS

MOMENTS OF DEFIANCE
3
STRIKES
A part of the workers' procession in Nairobi which took place on the 25th May 1937 during the strike.
BREAKING BARRIERS

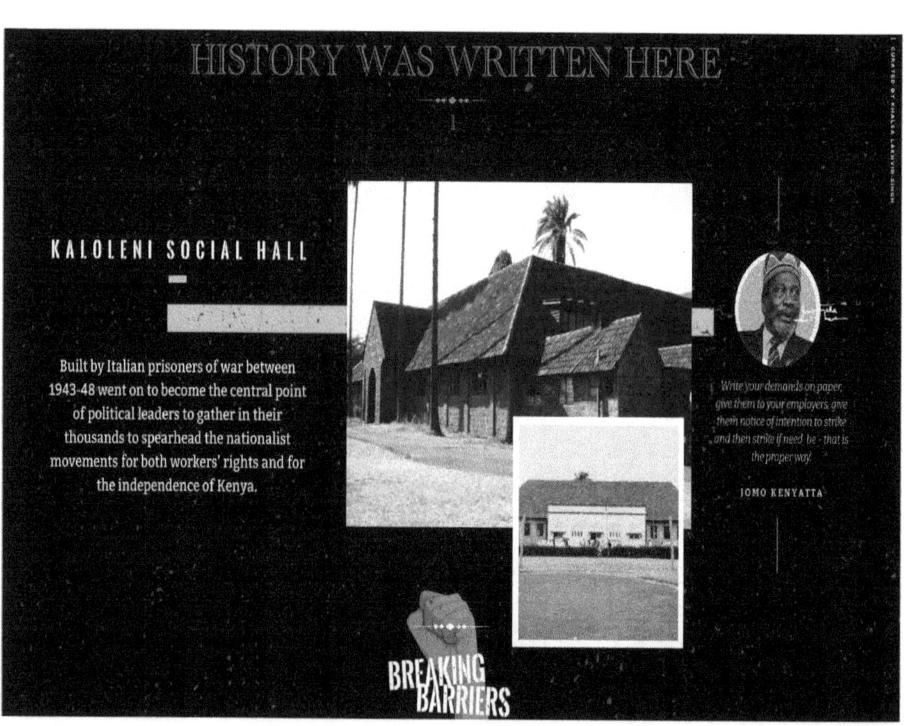
HISTORY WAS WRITTEN HERE
1
KALOLENI SOCIAL HALL
Built by Italian prisoners of war between 1943-48 went on to become the central point of political leaders to gather in their thousands to spearhead the nationalist movements for both workers' rights and for the independence of Kenya.
Write your demands on paper, give them to your employers, give them notice of intention to strike and then strike if need be - that is the proper way.
JOMO KENYATTA
BREAKING BARRIERS

A visual History by Makhan Singh
HISTORY WAS WRITTEN HERE
2
OFISI YA MASKINI TREE
The famous tree on the river bank of the Nairobi river where the meeting point of trade unionists revolutionaries was established in 1947.
Chege Kabachia addressed a meeting here at the African Workers Federation on the open ground near the Shauri Moyo bridge.

A visual History by Makhan Singh
HISTORY WAS WRITTEN HERE
4
SHAURI MOYO
Situated on the left bank of the Nairobi River where a fire ('moto moto') was lit during the 1950 General Strike and where workers' meetings used to be held.

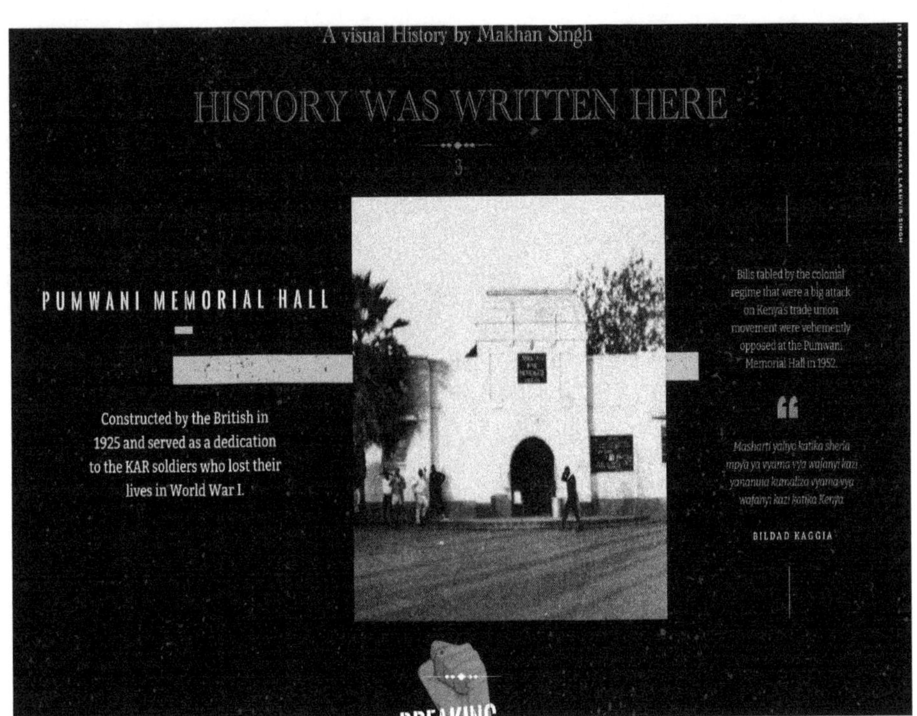
A visual History by Makhan Singh
HISTORY WAS WRITTEN HERE
3
PUMWANI MEMORIAL HALL
Constructed by the British in 1925 and served as a dedication to the KAR soldiers who lost their lives in World War I.
Bills tabled by the colonial regime that were a big attack on Kenya's trade union movement were vehemently opposed at the Pumwani Memorial Hall in 1952.
Masharti yaliyo katika sheria mpya ya vyama vya wafanyi kazi yananuia kumaliza vyama vya wafanyi kazi katika Kenya.
BILDAD KAGGIA

RETRACING TIME
1
1888
Imperial British East Africa Company founded
1891-1917
Several oppressive ordinances established against Africans
1895
British East Africa Protectorate established
1896
Uganda Railway construction started
1900
Uganda Railway strike by Indian and African workers
BREAKING

RETRACING TIME
2
1901
Uganda Railway completed
1902
African policmen go on strike in Mombasa
1908
African and Indian Railway workers strike in Mombasa
1912
African boat workers strike in Mombasa
1914
World War I begins. Indian and Africans strike.
BREAKING BARRIERS
CURATED BY KHALSA LAKHVIR-SINGH

RETRACING TIME
3
1919
Kikuyu Association formed, with Chief Koinange as leader
1920
Kenya Colony created
1921
Young Kikuyu Association founded by Harry Thuku
1927
Makhan Singh migrates to Kenya
1928
Jomo Kenyatta becomes secretary of Kikuyu Central Association
BREAKING

RETRACING TIME
4
1935
Makhan Singh transforms Indian Trade Union into the multi-racial Labour Trade Union of Kenya
1937
Trade Unions Ordinance passed to tame activities
1939
Series of strikes by Africans follow in Mombasa.
1940
Crack down on trade unions. Makhan Singh returns to India, arrested and detained by the British.
1942
World War II begins
BREAKING
BARRIERS

RETRACING TIME
5
1947
Makhan Singh sneaks back into Kenya. Organises massive Mombasa General Strike.
1950
Makhan Singh arrested in Nairobi and detained in Maralal.
1952
Jomo Kenyatta arrested in Nairobi and detained in Lodwar.
1961
Jomo Kenyatta released from detention, followed by Makhan Singh months after him.
1963
Kenya gains independence
BREAKING BARRIERS

MOMENTS IN HISTORY
1
TOGETHER AGAIN
Trade unions and independence struggle comrades **Achieng Oneko, Jomo Kenyatta and Oginga Odinga** reunite at the home of **Makhan Singh** in Nairobi after his release in 1961. They all endured colonial persecution for decades until Kenya finally gained independence in 1963.
BREAKING

MOMENTS IN HISTORY

2

UHURU SASA!

The rebellious African nationalists would gather often and relentlessly called for equal right for workers and for the immediate end to colonialism in Kenya. The trade union movement is what set the pace and the platform for independence for not just Kenya but for Uganda and Tanganyika as well.

BREAKING BARRIERS

CURATED BY KHALSA LAKHVIR-SINGH

MOMENTS IN HISTORY

3

UNITY OF PURPOSE

When it came to a common cause, barriers were broken down in every form - religion, colour, tribe or trade. That is what challenged and defeated those that used them for selfish gains.

CURATED BY KHALSA LAKHVIR-SINGH

MOMENTS IN HISTORY

4

CONTINUED SOLIDARITY

Makhan Singh with his comrades at the Printers & Kindred Trades Workers Union after his release from detention in 1961.

BREAKING

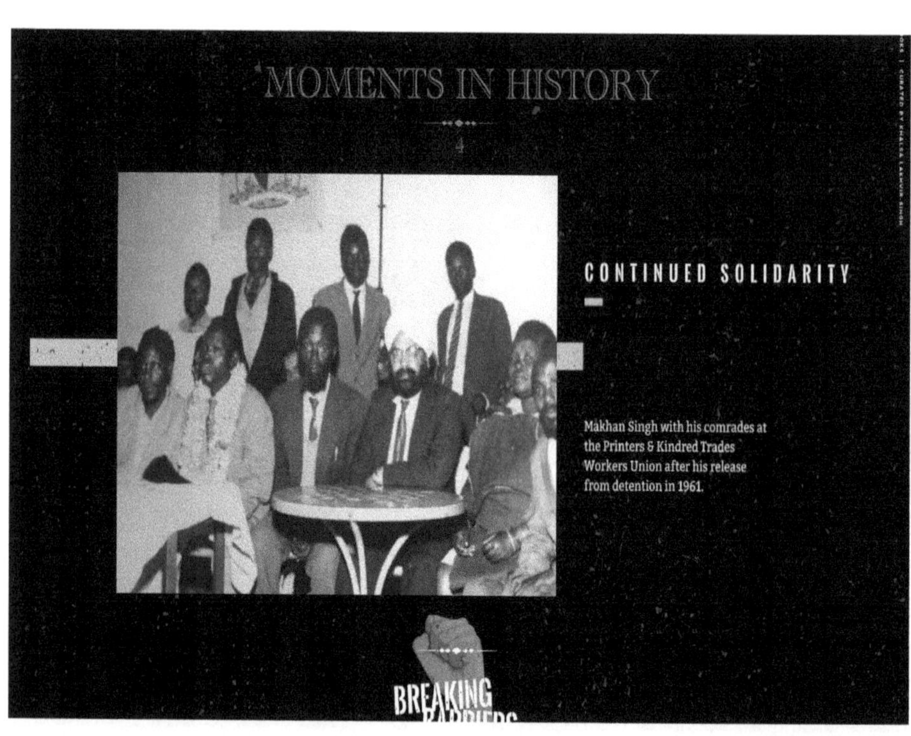

A visual History by Makhan Singh

MOMENTS IN HISTORY

5

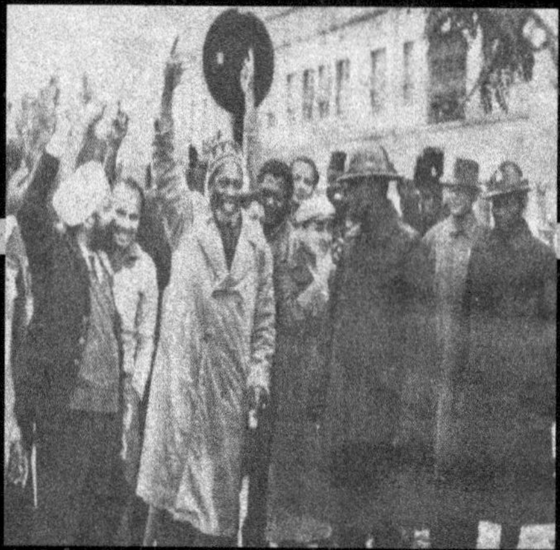

ONE BLOOD

Makhan Singh with Jomo Kenyatta, Tom Mboya and others celebrating a KANU victory.

Kenya's Trade Unions

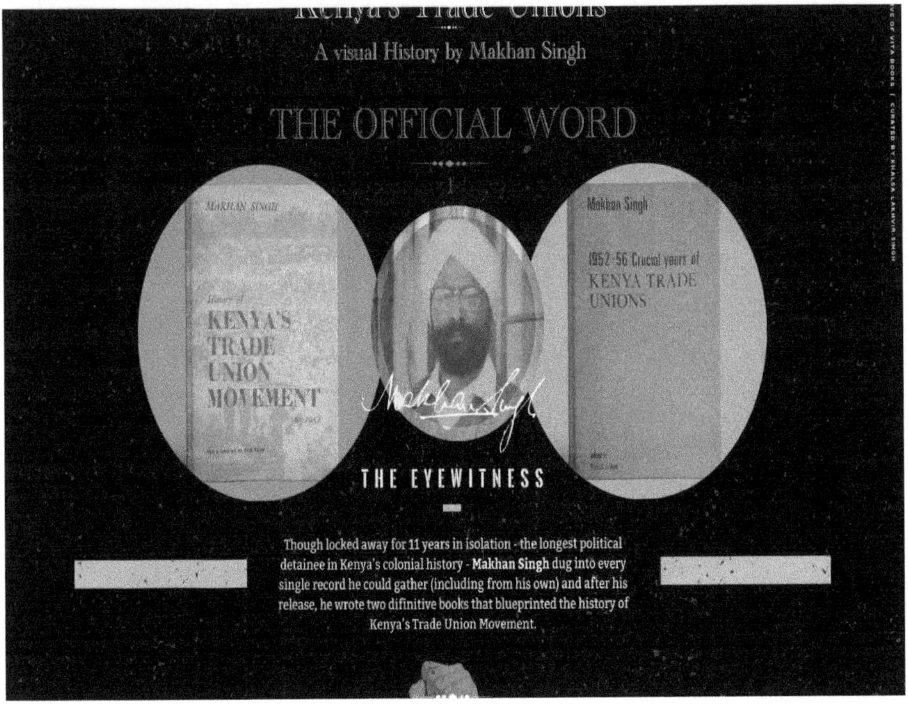

A visual History by Makhan Singh

THE OFFICIAL WORD

1

MAKHAN SINGH

History of KENYA'S TRADE UNION MOVEMENT

Makhan Singh

1952-56 Crucial years of KENYA TRADE UNIONS

THE EYEWITNESS

Though locked away for 11 years in isolation - the longest political detainee in Kenya's colonial history - **Makhan Singh** dug into every single record he could gather (including from his own) and after his release, he wrote two difinitive books that blueprinted the history of Kenya's Trade Union Movement.

A visual History by Makhan Singh
THE OFFICIAL WORD
2
AFTER MAKHAN SINGH
Though he never wrote about his own self but devoted himself to the African cause as an unadulterated idealist, a much deserved biography on him was published in a massive book by activist Zarina Patel - a once in a lifetime account of the man who was the centre of the trade unionism in Kenya as its pioneer and soul of the movement. More books were also written on both Makhan Singh and on other trade union history revolutionaries.
UNQUIET
THE LIFE & TIMES OF
MAKHAN SINGH
ZARINA PATEL
MAKHAN SINGH
62
DAYS
VITA BOOKS | CURATED BY KHALSA LAKHVIR-SINGH

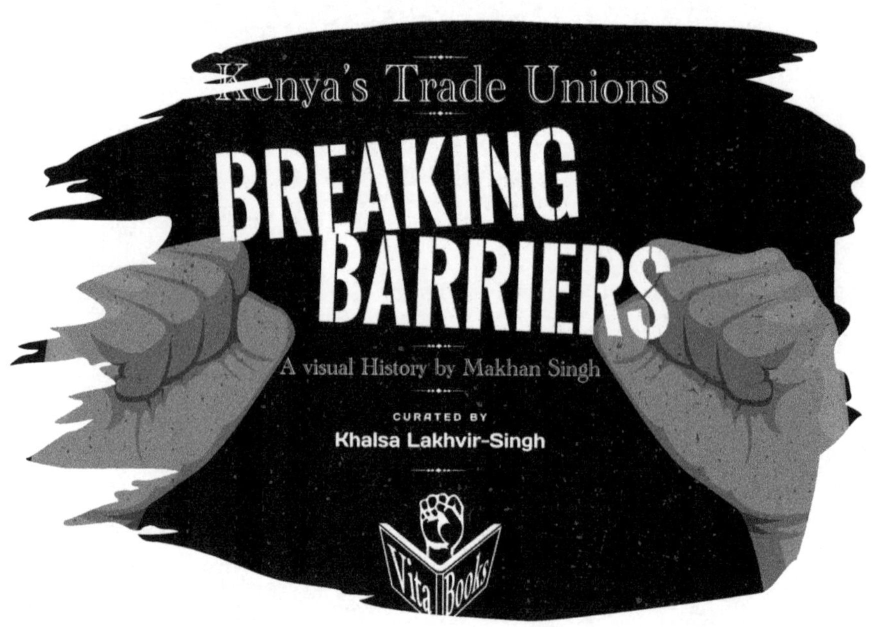
Kenya's Trade Unions
BREAKING
BARRIERS
A visual History by Makhan Singh
CURATED BY
Khalsa Lakhvir-Singh
Vita Books

Remembering Zarina Patel: 1935--2024

Vita Books and Ukombozi Library salute the memory of Zarina Patel, a writer, artist, human rights and race relations activist, environmentalist and campaigner for social justice. Zarina passed away in Nairobi on April 25, 2024.

Among her books was *Unquiet: The Life and Times of Makhan Singh* (2006) in which she explored Makhan Singh's childhood in India, his life outside his political concerns, the evolution of his politics, personality, and his experiences in detention. The research documented a hitherto un-researched archive of Singh's private papers, housed at the University of Nairobi.

VITA BOOKS

LIST OF BOOKS & PRICES (VAT EXCLUSIVE)

<table>
<tr>
<td>A STRUGGLE FOR RELEASE JOMO AND HIS COLLEAGUES
By Ambu H. Patel

2024
ISBN 978-9914-9777-5-8
Pages 238
Kshs. 2,000</td>
<td>TRADE UNION STUDIES IN UK AND KENYA by Nigel Flanagan & Shiraz Durrani

2024
ISBN 978-9914-9701-1-1
Pages 263
Kshs. 2000</td>
<td>A STRUGGLE OF 62 DAYS
By Shiraz Durrani
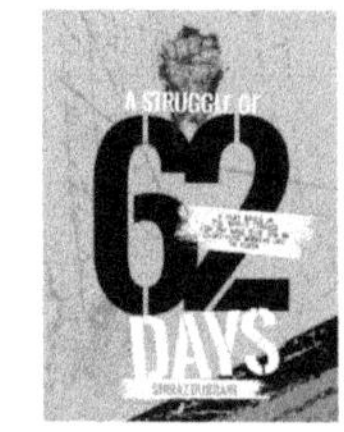
2024
ISBN 9789914970135
Pages 132
Kshs. 1,000</td>
<td>THE KENYA SOCIALIST
Edited by Shiraz Durrani & Kimani Waweru
No. 7

2023
ISBN 978-9914-9701-5-9
Pages 35
Kshs. 600</td>
</tr>
<tr>
<td>GUERRILLA INCURSIONS INTO THE CAPITALIST MINDSET
by Shiraz Durrani

2023
ISBN 978-9914-9701-9-7
Pages 451
Kshs. 2,500</td>
<td>THE KENYA SOCIALIST
Edited by Shiraz Durrani & Kimani Waweru
No. 6

2023
ISBN 978-9914-9621-0-9
Pages 60
Kshs. 600</td>
<td>THREADS OF TIME
The Ideological Struggle Between Capitalism and SoTorture, Imprisonment and a Quest for Social Justice
by Mugo Theuri

2023
ISBN 9789914962130
Pages 228
Kshs. 2,000</td>
<td>TWO PATHS AHEAD
The Ideological Struggle between Capitalism and Socialism in Kenya, 1960-1970
by Shiraz Durrani

2023
ISBN 978-9966-133-12-0
Pages 313
Kshs. 2,000</td>
</tr>
<tr>
<td>STRONGER THAN FAITH - My Journey in the Quest for Justice in Repressive Kenya - 1958- 2015
by Oduor Ong'wen

2022
ISBN 978-9914-9621-9-2
Pages 540
Kshs. 2,500</td>
<td>CABRAL PINTO
WILLY MUTUNGA UNDER COVER - Selected Opinion-Editorial Columns By Willy Mutunga Published Between 2006 and 2011

2022
ISBN 978-9914-9921-9-9
Pages 505
Kshs. 2,500</td>
<td>ANDOLO – The Talented Boy with Albinism
by Nsah Mala
Illustration – Akila Junior

2022
ISBN 987-9914-9921-7-5
Pages 28
Kshs. 500</td>
<td>THE KENYA SOCIALIST
Edited by Shiraz Durrani & Kimani Waweru
No. 5

2022
ISBN 978-9914-9921-1-3
Pages 39
Kshs. 600</td>
</tr>
</table>

KEY POINTS IN THE HISTORY OF KENYA,1885-1990 by Shiraz Durrani  2022 ISBN 978-9914-9875-7-7 Pages 158 Kshs. 1,200	THE KENYA SOCIALIST Edited by Shiraz Durrani & Kimani Waweru No. 4 2022 ISBN 978-9914-9921-1-4-4 Pages 39 Kshs. 600	ESSAYS ON PAN-AFRICANISM Edited by Shiraz Durrani & Noosim Naimasiah 2022 ISBN 978-9914-9875-6-0 Pages 271 Kshs. 2,000	THE KENYA SOCIALIST Edited by Shiraz Durrani & Kimani Waweru No. 3 2021 ISBN 9789914700893 Pages 40 Kshs. 600
THE STRUGGLE FOR LAND & JUSTICE IN KENYA by Ambreena Manji  2021 ISBN 978-9914-9875-8-4 Pages 208 Kshs. 2,500	ESCAPE FROM MONEYVILLE by Shiraz Durrani  2021 ISBN 9789914987508 Pages 69 Kshs. 800	NEITH ER SETTLER NOR NATIVE - The Making and Unmaking of Permanent Minorities by Mahmood Mamdani  2020 ISBN 9789914987546 Pages 401 Kshs. 2,500	THE KENYA SOCIALIST Edited by Shiraz Durrani & Kimani Waweru No. 2 2020 ISBN 9789914700893 Pages 26 Kshs. 600
CORPSES OF UNITY – An Anthology of Poems Edited by Nsah Mala & Mbizo Chirasha  2020 ISBN 9789966133991 Pages 105 Kshs. 1,000	CRIMES OF CAPITALISM IN KENYA - Press Cuttings on Moi-KANU's Reign of Terror in Kenya, 1980s-1990 Compiled by Shiraz Durrani & Kimani Waweru  2020 ISBN 9789966133113 Pages 224 Kshs. 1,500	THE KENYA SOCIALIST Edited by Shiraz Durrani & Kimani WaweruNo. 1  2019 ISBN 978-9966133816 Pages 37 Kshs. 600	PIO GAMA PINTO Kenya's Unsung Martyr. 1927 - 1965 Edited by Shiraz Durrani  2018 ISBN 9789966189004 Pages 391 Kshs. 2,200.00/=
MAU MAU THE REVOLUTIONARY, ANTI-IMPERIALIST FORCE FROM KENYA: 1948-1963 by Shiraz Durrani  2018 ISBN 9789966804020 Pages 154 Kshs. 800/=	TRADE UNIONS IN KENYA'S WAR OF INDEPENDENCE by Shiraz Durrani  2018 ISBN 9789966189097 Pages 118 Kshs. 800/=	PEOPLE'S RESISTANCE TO COLONIALISM AND IMPERIALISM IN KENYA by Shiraz Durrani  2018 ISBN 9789966114525 Pages 124 Kshs. 800/=	KENYA'S WAR OF INDEPENDENCE - Mau Mau and its Legacy of Resistance to Colonialism and Imperialism, 1948-1990 by Shiraz Durrani  2018 ISBN 9789966189011 Pages 450 Kshs. 2,000/=

<table>
<tr>
<td>LIBERATING MINDS, RESTORING KENYAN HISTORY - Anti-Imperialist Resistance by Progressive South Asian Kenyans 1884-1965 by Nazmi Durrani

2017
ISBN 9789966189097
Pages 202
Kshs. 800/=</td>
<td>MAKHAN SINGH. A Revolutionary Kenyan Trade Unionist
Edited by Shiraz Durrani
2016
ISBN 1869886135
Pages 194
Kshs. 1,500/=</td>
<td>PROGRESSIVE LIBRARIANSHIP
Perspectives from Kenya and Britain, 1979-2010
by Shiraz Durrani

2014
ISBN 9781869886202
Pages 446
Kshs. 2,000.00/=</td>
<td>INFORMATION AND LIBERATION
Writings on the Politics of Information and librarianship
by Shiraz Durrani

2008
ISBN 9789966189073
Pages 384
Kshs. 2,000.00/=</td>
</tr>
<tr>
<td>NEVER BE SILENT
Publishing and Imperialism in Kenya 1884-1963 by Shiraz Durrani

2008
ISBN 9789966189073
Pages 280
Kshs. 1,500.00/=</td>
<td>KARIMI NDUTHU: A Life in Struggle

1998
1869886127
Kshs. 300.00/=</td>
<td colspan="2">Vita Books are available at Ukombozi Library or from the following Bookshops
• Prestige Booksellers
• Bookstop, Yaya Centre
• Cheche Books & Coffee - Intertrade Africa
• Nuria Bookstore
• Chania Bookshop

Available Worldwide from African Books Collective
http://www.africanbookscollective.com/publishers/vitabooks</td>
</tr>
</table>

www.ingramcontent.com/pod-product-compliance
Ingram Content Group UK Ltd.
Pitfield, Milton Keynes, MK11 3LW, UK
UKHW022021190726
13853UKWH00005B/2046